Grace and Grit

Motorcycle Dispatches from Early Twentieth Century Women Adventurers

William M. Murphy

Arbutus Press
Traverse City, Michigan

Grace and Grit: Motorcycle Dispatches from Early Twentieth Century Woman © William M. Murphy 2012

ISBN 978-1-933926-40-7

Printed in the United States of America

Arbutus Press
Traverse City, Michigan
editor@arbutuspress.com
www.Arbutuspress.com

Library of Congress Cataloging-in-Publication Data
Murphy, William M. (William Martin), 1947–
Grace and grit : motorcycle dispatches from early twentieth century women adventurers / by
William M. Murphy.
p. cm.
Includes bibliographical references.
1. United States—Description and travel. 2. Women adventurers—United States—
Biography. 3. Women travelers—United States—Biography. 4. Motorcycle touring—United
States—History—20th century. 5. Women—Travel—United States—History—20th century.
I. Title.
E169.M968 2012
973.91—dc23
2011051801
ISBN 978-1-933926-40-7

Marseille 2017

Dedication

*To readers who have passion in their heart and wanderlust
in their blood, and who are capable of finding wonder
and amazement in everything they see.*

To Catherine,

With love + friendship.
Cheers to many more decades
of adventure here on Earth
+ Beyond.

xo Melissa

Table of Contents

—⟨∞⟩—

Prologue   1

Life in Early 20th Century America   3

The Amazing Engine That Could   8

America Hits the Road   19

America's Love Affair With Motorcycles   36

Victorian Girls Breaking All the Rules   50

Della Crewe: A Small Town Girl With Big Dreams   64

The Great Adventure of Effie and Avis Hotchkiss   92

The Van Buren Sisters: Out to Change America   140

Epilogue   197

Time Table   201

References   205

Acknowledgements

A book such as this is never written in a vacuum. The help and cooperation of many individuals, organizations, and institutions is required. I am deeply grateful for the support and assistance provided to me during the research for this book. I especially want to thank the following people and organizations:

First and foremost; Publisher Susan Bays of Arbutus Press, LLC, for her faith in me.

Mr. Craig Dove; Mrs. Barbara Dove; and Robert & Rhonda Van Buren; proud descendants of some of the stars of the book, and sources of valuable information and pictures. The cooperation of these families was of great importance in making this a successful venture. I appreciate their trust.

Also special thanks to: Ms. Maggie Humberston of the City of Springfield Indian Motorcycle Museum; The Antique Motorcycle Club of America; The Harley-Davidson Museum; The National Motorcycle Museum; The Missouri Historical Society; Ms. Lesley Niblett and the Ninety-Nines Inc. Museum; The Oldsmobile Museum; and The Lincoln Highway Association.

Assistance by reference and historical collection librarians in the following locations was also invaluable: Colorado Springs, Ute Pass, and Grand Junction, CO; Terre Haute, IN; City of Des Moines and Cowles Library / Drake University, IA; Springfield and Worcester, MA; City of Detroit / Burton Historical Collection, East Lansing, Lansing, University of Michigan / Bentley Library, & the State of Michigan Library, MI; Omaha, Kearney, & North Platte, NE; Ely & Elko, NV; Erie, PA; Buffalo, Newburgh, & Syracuse, NY; Akron, Ashtabula, Cleveland, and Toledo, OH; Green River & the Utah State Library, UT; Milwaukee, WI. And thanks to Carol Swinehart for editing assistance.

Most importantly, I am appreciative of the support and patience of my family, who put up with my many weeks on the road for more than a year while conducting research for the book.

Life in Early 20th Century America

—◦⁄◦⁄◦—

How ya gonna keep 'em down on the farm
After they've seen Paree'
How ya gonna keep 'em away from Broadway
Jazzin around and paintin' the town
How ya gonna keep 'em away from harm, that's a mystery
They'll never want to see a rake or plow
And who the deuce can parleyvous a cow?
How ya gonna keep 'em down on the farm
After they've seen Paree[1]

What an amazing time to have been alive! For many Americans, the period preceding the country's entry into World War I was one of unbridled excitement and seemingly endless possibilities. The Gay Nineties had morphed into the 20th century and a new age had dawned, one that promised to transform everything. Nearly every facet of life was changing in ways that had not been seen since the dawn of human history.

The telephone, electricity, radiotelegraphy, electric lights, and advances in health care were becoming a part of everyday life for millions. Peculiar new words such as refrigerator, vacuum cleaner, records, Victrola, X-ray, and the strange new lingo associated with the automobile, became part of the everyday lexicon. For the first time, machines could carry people almost anywhere they wished to go, and vehicles

---

[1] *How Ya Gonna Keep Them Down on the Farm.* Lyrics by Lewis and Young. Music by Walter Donaldson. Produced by Waterson, Berlin & Snyder Company, New York. 1919

3

capable of flying through the air became a reality, fulfilling mankind's dream of flight. People born around 1890 witnessed a remarkable period of technological and societal change.

All sections of the economy saw improvement and the new wonders that were appearing in every aspect of life were no longer primarily the domain of the wealthy. Egalitarian benefits of this new world order were within the grasp of the working class more than at any time in history. The ability to finally break loose from centuries-old constraints created an optimistic belief that a better life lay ahead for the children and grandchildren of immigrants in a new country.

THE ECONOMIC BOON of the early 20th century resulted in greater disposable income for many workers. Goods of every description were in demand, and America found itself as the world's principal manufacturer of many of these products. Consumers, workers, and manufacturers were in an epic economic dance, the scope and impact of which the world had never known. It was a fortuitous alignment of the stars; more opportunities for employment, increased pay levels, shorter work hours with more time for recreational activities, and higher quality, more dependable products available at lower cost. It's no wonder that the American consumer was in a buying mood.

Beginning in 1914 Henry Ford reduced the work day to eight hours and paid an unheard of wage of five dollars for each of those days. Mechanization meant less back-breaking labor and increased productivity, which led to shorter work weeks and weekends off to spend on recreational pursuits—another pioneering concept. These advancements marked a dramatic shift in how the average person lived, and many families now had the means to consider purchases beyond the bare basics.

The period of roughly 1895 to 1920 would become known as the Progressive Era with good reason. The welfare of the working class was in the forefront of national debates regarding economic policies, and the plight of workers was improving. Manufacturing prowess resulted in the availability of a wide variety of goods at prices that the emerging middle class could afford. These developments created the world's most powerful consumer economy, and many Americans were gladly jumping on this new century's economic bandwagon.

Because of rapidly improving circumstances and opportunities the early 20th century was filled with a sense of adventure and unlimited possibilities for many Americans. Citizens began to view the world differently; from the context of possibilities, rather than merely the basic necessities of life. The opportunities created by the social and economic developments of a century ago allowed people to consider options and activities that would simply have been unavailable a generation earlier.

It was a time of energetic no-holds-barred economic competition and high-tech progress. Barely was one record set, or an invention reached the hands of consumers, before an improved version appeared. This was true in every facet of life, from the telephone to recorded music, and from motorcycles to airplanes. It was truly an exciting time to be alive. America was on the springboard of a bright future that promised undreamed of benefits for rich and poor. Prospects seemed bright indeed, whether viewed from the individual or national perspective.

A NEW WAY of thinking about what it meant to be American also dawned along with the new century's economic and social developments. President Theodore Roosevelt helped establish a sense of nationalistic confidence and can-do optimism with his personal style and charisma, his attitudes about living life large, and through his extension of American power and influence beyond the country's borders for the first time. He established a new definition of America's national destiny and catapulted the country onto the world stage like never before.

The charismatic President held that a country could only be as strong and capable as its citizens. Accordingly, he advocated that Americans challenge themselves to develop a strong character and healthy bodies, as he himself had done. He lived his philosophy that "manly" pursuits separate the strong and successful from the weak and unworthy.

With the end of rugged frontier life and the development of large cities, and with the transition of labor from strenuous outdoor work to factory and sedentary office settings, Roosevelt feared that America and her citizens would grow soft and undisciplined. He campaigned vigorously for what he called "the strenuous life" because he believed that a citizenry that pushed itself to excel would give America a sharp edge and make the country stronger.

Roosevelt's philosophy influenced the raising of a new generation of the nation's youth. Parents across the country heeded his advice and exposed their offspring to arduous outdoor activities. Young people enthusiastically followed Roosevelt's lead and pursued lives of adventure and challenge. There is little question that Roosevelt's words had an impact on the women who are the subject of this book. Their upbringing and outlook on life reflected the kind of healthy, daring, and active lifestyle that he preached.

Presidential pronouncements go only so far, however. As it turned out, conditions and circumstances in America a century ago were well suited to forge the fundamental characteristics necessary to pursue ideas and take chances. Attitudes of self-sufficiency and confidence in those who chased dreams during this era are perhaps the most endearing qualities they possessed. Whether simply living their daily lives or pursuing an adventure, citizens of the early 20th century accepted the challenges and carried the load without expectation of help or pity. They knew that the path would be difficult and the obstacles many, but they possessed a marvelous can-do attitude that allowed them to accept the difficulties in their path and press on regardless. These characteristics are abundantly apparent in the subjects of this book.

AFTER COMMENCEMENT of hostilities in 1914, Americans argued loud and long about the war waging across Europe. Many genuinely felt that the country had no business getting involved in the "War to End All Wars". Others felt that involvement in the European war was inevitable and that we were putting our nation's security at risk by burying our collective heads in the sand. The First World War lacked the clear moral and legal principles that garnered public support for World War II, and many people did not support either side in the early years. As with other conditions and sentiments of the early part of last century, the war, looming as it did like a dark cloud just over the horizon, affected the thinking and plans of many young Americans during the period. The lives of almost all the women whose stories are told in the following chapters would have been very different but for the war. Consciously or not it affected who they were and what they did.

Sentiment against Germany eventually coalesced when a German U-boat sank the passenger steamship RMS Lusitania in May 1915, killing nearly 1,200 civilians. America ultimately entered the war in April, 1917 to protect shipping on the high seas and to come to the aid of France and Great Britain.

In the absence of radio, television, and the Internet, news traveled more slowly, but citizens read daily newspapers to follow the fluid and perilous situations facing average Americans. Most cities of any size had morning and evening newspapers so that people could stay abreast of major events. Even small town papers carried international news stories because they were generally the only source of information. Thus, in towns such as Peoria, one could read about what neighbors were doing, whom they were visiting, who had died, and who was marrying whom, as well as follow the progress of the war in Europe with daily battlefield updates.

All in all, life in 1910s America was an intoxicating mix of worry and promise, urban slums and hilltop mansions, hope and despair, and progress and the loss of dignity, in some cases, because of that progress. War and peace struggled to co-exist. New industries, inventions, and miracle chemicals resulted in promises of a better life, but also in unwanted and unexpected consequences. And through it all people lived their daily lives and chased their dreams.

The Amazing Engine That Could

⟞◦⟊◦⟝

And the little old Ford, it rambled right along,
And the little old Ford, it rambled right along,
The gas burned out in the big machine.
But the darn little Ford don't need gasoline.
the big limousine had to back down hill.
The blamed little Ford is going up still.
When she blows out a tire,
Just wrap it up with wire
And the little Ford will ramble right along.[1]

As much as any other single factor, the development of the internal combustion engine enabled citizens to break away from ways of life that had prevailed among human beings from the beginning of time through the end of the 19th century. The transition from flesh and blood horsepower to another power source—created by a spark igniting a combustible mixture within a cylinder, driving down a piston and turning a crankshaft—changed everything.

This new source of power was available to most people—rich or poor, educated or uneducated, farmer or industrialist, banker or politician—and no one would remain untouched by its many far-reaching ramifications. The engine reduced backbreaking work on the most isolated farms and created well-paid factory jobs in the heart of our cities.

---

1 *The Little Ford Rambled Right Along*. Lyrics by Foster and Gay, performed by Billy Murray, © 1914 the CR Foster Publishing Co, Los Angeles, California.

Because of the internal combustion engine many people became millionaires, and thousands of workers became part of a middle class the likes of which the world had never witnessed before. The engine's very existence produced wealth through its manufacture, and along every strand of the web of economic pathways created by its many uses. This paradigm-changing invention armed a revolution in the way citizens in all levels of society worked and lived, and of how people saw themselves and their possibilities in the larger world.

No sooner had the internal combustion engine been bolted into a carriage than inventors and innovators saw how it could be improved. And improvements came rapidly. Frank and Charles Duryea built the first automobile in America in 1893 in Springfield, Massachusetts. It was powered by an anemic single-cylinder engine. Within two years the brothers figured out how to build a significantly more powerful two-cylinder engine that allowed a top speed of seven miles per hour.

The stage was set for another American revolution in the ownership and use of vehicles propelled by the internal combustion engine. Like the Revolution of 1776, this latter day movement was also motivated by a desire for freedom. Americans of every class wanted the independence and myriad benefits that this new technology provided.

The introduction of the automobile into American life as it existed in the early 1900s was not without considerable strain on the social order that had been the norm for centuries. The automobile affected every aspect of society and culture, for good or ill, and it was anything but a smooth transition from the old to the new. Many people did not welcome the smelly, noisy, smoke-belching early cars and certainly didn't see them as an advancement of civilization.

Americans in the 1910s were driving on the same trails that their ancestors rode across in stagecoaches and covered wagons. Some buildings still had signs identifying them as stagecoach stops, and blacksmith shops far outnumbered automobile repair facilities. It was truly a fascinating mix of the old and the rapidly-advancing new, and conflicts between the old lifestyle and the latest inventions were common. More horses than motorized vehicles were on the nation's roads in the first decade of the 20th century, and these strange new contraptions frightened horses, causing many accidents with runaway teams and bucking steeds.

A chance meeting of two cars crossing the vast Nevada desert circa 1915. Early automobile travelers used the same trails carved out of the wilderness by pioneers in covered wagons during their westward migration. In the deserts of the Great Basin these vague trails often disappeared altogether, and meeting another traveler in these desolate locations was always a pleasant, sometimes a life saving, occurrence. (Used with the permission of the University of Michigan / Bentley Library)

The ramifications of this new motorized age were many and varied. Since the dawn of time, humans had lived in settings where loud noise was something out of the ordinary. For thousands of years, people were immersed in the silence that surrounded their hunter/gatherer existence in the wilderness, or in the pastoral peacefulness of subsistence agriculture. Natural noises were all that interrupted the stillness in the vast rural spaces of America.

Only when gunpowder was invented did loud, manmade noises intrude. For three hundred more years, the occasional gunshot, cannon fire, or fireworks broke the silence, but, for the most part, humans lived in a quiet world where the clip clop of horse's hooves on dirt trails or the sound of the human voice prevailed. That all suddenly ended with the introduction of the horseless carriage.

Without warning, the silence that had existed since the beginning of time was tainted with the obnoxious snarl of early automobiles and motorized two-wheel cycles. Barely muffled, these vehicles emitted an ear-splitting noise that shattered the calm and left in their wake a smoky odor that hung in the air long after they were gone. A galloping team of horses could raise some dust, but a car roaring down city streets left a plume of thick dust that covered everything and everybody in its wake.

Perhaps worst of all, drivers handled their cars in such a manner that the streets were suddenly unsafe for the casual pedestrian. Humans and horses had long enjoyed a mutually beneficial relationship, with humans taking care of their equine charges and the steeds being loyal and obedient to their masters. A speeding car offered no such courtesies; when a child nonchalantly walked out in front of one, the results were tragic.

Early automobile owners' speeding and reckless driving was a very real problem, and local officials had every reason to be concerned. The motorized vehicle phenomenon exploded after 1910 with the advent of mass production. Self-propelled vehicles were no longer a novelty, as cars had become less expensive, more powerful, and more dependable. Their critics gradually realized that, despite their wishes, the motorized vehicles weren't just a fad destined to fade away after a few years. There would be no return to their "normal," centuries-old way of life dictated by the speed and abilities of horse-drawn conveyances.

Furthermore, automobiles and their uses were only minimally regulated, and virtually anyone could drive one. Newspapers of the era are filled with stories of people killed when drivers lost control of their speeding cars and struck innocent bystanders, hit objects such as trees and telephone poles, or rolled over from driving too fast for conditions.

Early vehicles lacked the sophistication and engineering of later cars. Coupled with roads that were often little more than narrow, tree-lined dirt paths, not designed for speed above that of a trotting horse, it was a recipe for disaster. The rate of persons killed in car accidents, based on either the number of cars on the road or overall human population, was vastly higher then than today.

For example, Ohio, a typical state both then and now, recorded 404 traffic fatalities in 1916, according to the 1917 *Ohio Public Health Journal*, at a time when approximately 114,000 vehicles were driven on its roads—one car for every 44 citizens. Today 12 million cars are driven on Ohio's crowded roads—slightly more than one car for each resident—and the number of miles driven is immeasurably higher. If the same accident rate held true today as for 1916, well over 42,000 traffic fatalities would happen in Ohio each year! Fortunately, the accident rate has dropped dramatically since those wild days, and the number killed in vehicular accidents today in the Buckeye State is closer to 1,300 per year.

In an attempt to improve the driving habits of motorized vehicles, it was commonplace for communities to enact restrictive laws governing the use and speed limits of cars and motorcycles, even on the open roads between towns. Ohio and Nebraska were two of many states that had 20 mph speed limits on rural roads with few homes or other vehicles of any kind. These laws were less for the safety of drivers than for the tranquility and protection of residents who lived along the roads or who traveled on them in horse-drawn buggies.

Local police and justices of the peace had little sympathy for anyone they felt was operating a two- or four-wheeler in a manner that disturbed the peace of humans or animals. Judges handed down some severe sentences to violators, and newspaper articles about drivers who were fined for driving in a manner that threatened public safety were quite common.

Enforcement officers frequently targeted loud cars or motorcycles that disturbed the equine peace. Spooked horses, and their unpredictable responses, were serious problems. If a horse were frightened because of a loud vehicle, the car or motorcycle owner would almost certainly be cited into court.

Could it be that the horse knew that its time was limited and sometimes got revenge? A common problem a century ago was flat tires caused by horseshoe nails lying on the streets and trails. Farmers also extracted retribution and maintained a sense of superiority over travelers who came to their doors requesting help to pull their car out of a mud hole with a team of horses.

Many cities hired additional police officers and often put them on motorcycles, which seemed to comprise a larger part of the law enforcement fleet circa 1915 than they do today. Many articles from contemporary media make reference to motorcycles used for police work across the country and in all four seasons. Undoubtedly, the ability to take two-wheelers places where early cars couldn't go made them excellent machines for police work.

Of course, drivers complained about overzealous law enforcement and receiving tickets. Writing tickets on a commission basis may have been behind some of this. *Motor Cycle Illustrated* magazine reported that East Youngstown, Ohio, hired a motor officer in 1917 to fight the menace of speeding there, and he received a commission for each apprehension. The more tickets he wrote, the higher his take home pay. An effective method to be sure, but probably not the best approach to insure that justice was well served.

Mrs. Harriet White Fisher of Trenton, New Jersey, was possibly a victim of this sort of enforcement. After becoming a widow at age 35, Fisher became a world-class traveler with few peers. A daring woman, in 1910 and 1911 she and her nephew covered large parts of several continents in her Locomobile, including a trip from the Pacific to the Atlantic in America. In 1911 she wrote a book called *A Woman's World Tour in a Motor* describing her adventure. In it she told of an incident in Sandusky, Ohio, that seems to have been a clear example of enforcement for the sake of enhanced salary, rather than for public safety.

A motorcycle officer pulled her over and accused her of speeding. She contended that they were going only 15–18 miles per hour in a 20 mph speed zone and that the officer was mistaken. At that point, he suggested that some "remuneration" would set things right, but Mrs. Fisher was having nothing to do with bribes. This was a matter of principle, and she was not going to acquiesce to paying that price simply for the sake of expediency. After appearing before the local judge, who exhibited none of the normal judicial decorum we expect today, Mrs. Fisher found that she was not going to receive an impartial hearing and eventually paid a fine.

Fisher's impression that she did not get a fair shake in the criminal justice system of Sandusky was almost certainly not just sour grapes. She went into the courtroom with two strikes against her. Not only was it the officer's word against hers, but she likely encountered in the judge an example of many older Americans of the time. Such people viewed automobiles, and those with the means to own and tour with them, with disdain.

The prickly relationship between drivers and police has existed for as long as motorized vehicles have been on the road, and the concept of writing tickets for infractions extends back more than a hundred years. The first traffic ticket in America was reportedly written in 1904 in Dayton, Ohio, though this is one of those historic "facts" that is hard to document. The cat and mouse game of speeders trying to avoid apprehension, and police trying to apprehend speeders, had begun.

An organization called the Safety First Federation of America formed in 1915 to lobby for uniform vehicle and traffic laws. Its goals included a nationwide requirement for licensing all drivers, requiring that applicants actually demonstrate their physical and mental qualifications to operate a vehicle. In a forward-looking recommendation, they also lobbied for states to require a photograph of the licensee so that police could be sure that the person was who s/he claimed to be.

Although the requirement to register vehicles had its beginnings in 1901, the licensing of drivers per se was a hit-or-miss concept. Massachusetts and Missouri led the way in 1903 by requiring a permit to operate a motorized vehicle on public roadways, but it was without restriction and required simply paying a small fee. It wasn't until 1913 that New Jersey required drivers to actually take and pass both written and driving tests. This approach caught on slowly, however. As late as the 1940s and 1950s some states still issued a driver's license without the requirement to prove one's ability to drive.

ALL LAWS OF HUMAN NATURE would have been violated had not the earliest car and motorcycle owners attempted to see whose motorized vehicle was the fastest. Racing—involving chariots, horseback riders, runners, boats and ships, and, no doubt, every other conveyance ever used by humans—had been going on for millennia.

Racing of every form soon swept across the nation, and competition wasn't limited to the race tracks. Simply travelling long distances over the dirt trails that passed as roads became competitive events. Endurance races—from dozens to several hundred miles long—were held on roads that connected cities and towns. They were in such poor condition that no special course was necessary; most of them in their natural state presented all the hazards and difficult sections one could desire in endurance runs.

This 1916 R.E. Olds 2-cylinder Model L, manufactured in Lansing, Michigan, was considered a high quality luxury car, despite its lack of protection from the weather. (Photo by author)

The first publicized race between automobiles, what was in effect the earliest endurance run, took place in 1895. By then several manufacturers were researching different technologies, including electric cars. The *Chicago Times-Herald* sponsored the 54-mile race down the muddy trails near Chicago to see which car was the fastest and most reliable. It took over ten hours, but the Duryea twin-cylinder vehicle was the first to cross the finish line, with an average speed of 7.3 miles per hour. Of the six cars in the race, only two finished.

Another early endurance competition was a 500-mile contest between New York City and Buffalo sponsored by the Automobile Club of America, held in September 1901. Seventy cars left New York City on September 9, and the race was cancelled at Syracuse five days later due to President McKinley's assassination. The most noteworthy feature of the run was mud. New York State's roads were better than most as long as it didn't rain. But rain it did… in torrents. *The Motor Way Journal* described roads across the Mohawk Valley as "rivers of greasy, slimy mud and broken at intervals by pools of water into which the motor carriages sunk hub deep."

Within just a few years, the sport of motor vehicle racing took hold. The first track dedicated specifically to car racing was the Milwaukee Mile, an oval course that began life as a horse racing venue but, beginning in 1903, also hosted car and motorcycle races. To the delight and amazement of spectators, cars and motorcycles roared with abandon around courses that sprang up across the nation. Within just a few years, closed track car and motorcycle racing was very common.

By 1910 two main groups of motorized competitors had emerged—those who strove for speed and those who drove for distance. Men and women who faced the idol of speed became the matadors who gladly risked life and limb for the honor of being part of a tiny group basking in the adulation bestowed on sports heroes. The contests quickly became more extreme and dangerous and many of these competitors fell before the bull. The danger and speed only served to make the followers even more enthusiastic.

Manufacturers eventually sponsored race teams comprised of the best talent, which served to raise the bar on quality racing even higher. But such sponsorship had other benefits for manufacturers. Racing and competition served two important functions in the early days of motorized vehicles; research and development, and advertising. There was simply no better way to test a product, or a design idea, than full out on the race track.

Racers were willing to risk it all for the fame and upward social and economic mobility that they could achieve through this hot new profession. In turn, they pushed machines to the ultimate and quickly discovered any flaws in vehicle or engine design, then brought them to the attention of company engineers.

Corporate officials also quickly learned the value of racing for product sales and brand loyalty. Spectators not only wanted to see an exciting race, they wanted to see the brand they were loyal to, and probably owned, win. And winning races was a sure way to make believers out of undecided potential customers.

Riders such as Ray Weishaar, Leslie "Red" Parkhurst, Floyd Clymer, Otto Walker, and Erwin "Cannonball" Baker were among a select fraternity that enjoyed fame and many loyal fans during their usually short racing careers. The NASCAR phenomenon of the 21st century has nothing on the wildly enthusiastic and faithful following of individual racers and their brand of machine of a century ago. "Win on Sunday, Sell on Monday" was as true an axiom for auto and motorcycle manufacturers then as it is today.

Long distance endurance races also remained very popular, though much less of a spectator sport. Because the United States stretched across the continent between two oceans, it is understandable that an enthusiastic desire to travel from coast to coast also evolved as soon as the self-propelled vehicle appeared on the scene. Two-wheeled enthusiasts will proudly inform anyone who asks that the first transcontinental crossing by way of a motorized vehicle was on a motorcycle. A bicycling enthusiast named George Wyman rode a 90cc 1.25 horsepower California brand motorcycle from San Francisco to New York City. Wyman left the west coast on May 16, 1903, and arrived in New York on July 6, for a crossing time of 50 days.

WYMAN PRECEDED THE first crossing by automobile by just a few days. On May 23, 1903, Dr. H. Nelson Jackson and Sewall Crocker also left San Francisco to attempt a cross-country drive in a car. It took them 63 days to drive a 1903 Winton automobile from the west coast to the east, arriving in New York City on July 26.

After these first crossings, various people threw their hats in the ring to up the ante. During the 1903–1916 period, newspapers and magazines followed and reported on transcontinental excursions, even though they were considered less exciting and less dangerous than high speed racing events. This publicity fueled interest, and the race was on to make the crossing faster or to be the first to make the crossing under different conditions, routes, and vehicle types. And it wasn't just men who got caught up in the competitive frenzy for long distance jaunts. Many women autoists (as early automobile owners were called) and bikers alike enthusiastically joined the fray.

By the mid-1910s the competitive edge of long distance travel had been dulled. Many men and several women had driven cars from coast to coast, and it was no longer a notable accomplishment. Cross-country trips by automobile had become quite commonplace, though not necessarily easy or guaranteed to succeed.

While several women had attempted ocean-to-ocean trips on motorcycles, as of 1914 none had made it all the way. This was the last frontier. In their own way and for their own reasons, women such as the Van Buren sisters, Effie and Avis Hotchkiss, Della Crewe, and several others decided to attempt what hadn't been done before. Their routes, destinations, purposes, and end results may have differed, but they all shared one quality; they did what many people said they could not or should not do.

Those closest to these adventurers had good reason to caution them about pursuing their dreams. They were proposing something that was challenging at best and not without real dangers. Driving across the continent in a car could be difficult, but it was doable. Crossing the country on a motorcycle was a much greater challenge.

Poor roads and lack of services for travelers were just two of the conditions which demonstrated that America was just barely removed from the frontier era of one generation earlier. Much of the country was little changed from the land that the children of the wagon trains experienced, and the wild west of the 19th century was still very much alive in some places. The *Springfield Daily Republican* reported that, on July 5, 1916, a bandit riding a horse robbed four stagecoaches carrying tourists near Wawona, California, just outside Yosemite National Park. It may have been the twentieth century but not all traces of the frontier had been erased.

America Hits the Road

———◁●◇●▷———

Gasoline! Gasoline!
Ev'rywhere you go you smell it,
Ev'ry motor seems to yell it.
Gasoline! Gasoline!
That's the cry that echoes thru your dreams.
Gasoline! Gasoline!
In this land of milk and honey
'Tisn't love—isn't money
Rules the world, now ain't it funny?
Gasoline! Gasoline![1]

In the first decade of the 20th century the horseless carriage wasn't taken very seriously. Most people thought that cars were an ostentatious, and passing, fad of rich men who had excess time and money on their hands. Horse-drawn conveyances outnumbered the rare motorized vehicle on remote roads circa 1910. *American Motorist* magazine, a popular journal that covered the burgeoning automobile and travel phenomenon in the new century's early years, reported that one car per week crossed the continent in 1910. That was to change quickly, but this extremely low number paints an accurate picture that motorized travel was very much still the exception.

---

[1] Lyrics by J. Will Callahan, music composed by Paul Pratt. Published 1913 by Frank Root & Co., Chicago.

The earliest cars were undependable, cantankerous, and certainly not user-friendly. Auto owners spent an inordinate amount of time under their vehicles, repairing various broken parts or changing flat tires rather than sitting in the driver's seat enjoying the ride. Even when their automobile was running satisfactorily, they always had to be ready, with shovel and tow rope nearby, to extricate themselves from ever-present mud holes.

Hand cranks made the vehicles hard to start, and concern about a backfire and what that meant to one's arm and wrist kept many people, and virtually all women, from owning a car. A newspaper account of injuries received by a Salt Lake City police commissioner's chauffeur was typical of what often happened. The story described how the engine backfired as the driver was cranking it, with the crank hitting him on the side of the face and causing serious injuries. It was only because this particular man was a police commissioner's driver that his plight made the papers. The same sort of injury occurred across the land, with broken thumbs or sprained wrists being particularly commonplace.

Having spent a childhood on a farm with three tractors that required hand-cranking, I can attest to the very unpleasant surprise you get when an engine backfires as you try to turn it over with a crank. You quickly learn tricks to try to lessen the impact of a backfire, but no one can avoid the result of a crank suddenly sent spinning in the opposite direction.

However, automobiles improved rapidly. Cadillac installed the first electric starter in 1912, and other manufacturers soon followed suit. By 1915 the electric starter was an option available on many models, and by 1920 almost all cars came equipped with the starter that has been standard equipment ever since.

Events that impacted motorized travel were coalescing in the pre-World War I period in America, while the events themselves were being influenced simultaneously by motorized travel developments. The European war affected Americans in ways that went far beyond typical geopolitical and military implications. Since the late 1890s Europe had been the place where the rich and famous took their automobiles for touring. European roads were far ahead of their American counterparts, and one could travel by car in comfort on smooth roads, and look forward to posh restaurants and hotels at day's end. It was a magical period for those who could afford to participate, but beginning in 1914 Europe was off-limits to autoists.

However, these folks were not about to sell their fancy cars and turn back the clock. They now looked for driving opportunities in their own country to satisfy their sense of adventure. The "See America First" movement swept the nation, exhorting Americans to discover their own country's many attractions, which the majority of people had not seen or explored.

Automobile technology progressed at an incredible rate in its first twenty years. By the second decade of the 20th century, autos had earned the respect of even the most ardent detractors, and they quickly became a common sight on America's roads. The era of the horse had finally come to an end. The number of automobiles, on the other hand, exploded.

By January 1, 1916, an estimated 2,225,000 motor vehicles were being driven on America's roads and parked in driveways, barns and sheds of every description, according to estimates of the Federal Trade Commission. (The concept of residential garages hadn't yet caught on.) Today's number is approximately 250 million, a 112-fold increase.

Early automobile buyers had a dizzying array of manufacturers and models to choose from, as companies churned out cars to satisfy the needs and incomes of car buyers across the economic spectrum. Equally important, a national network of dealers and technicians quickly sprang up to repair their cars and supply parts when needed. The trained automobile mechanic began to replace the local blacksmith as the person car owners could count on to fix their vehicles.

The missing important ingredient in America's blossoming love affair with the automobile was roads upon which to operate these marvelous machines. In the four decades between the Civil War and the turn of the century, the railroad became the primary means of transportation in America. Roads were local affairs, connecting small towns and providing a means for farmers to get their produce to towns and rail shipping points. Few people had the time or money to travel long distances for pleasure, and if they needed to travel to a distant location they got on a train.

Railroads dominated interstate transportation of people and goods, relegating roads to a second-class status. The rail network in the latter 19th and early 20th centuries was a masterpiece of planning and technology. Rail mileage hit its peak in 1916 with 254,000 miles of track. All portions of the country were linked, and railroads served the needs of the country as they existed at that time. By the 1850s railroads had sounded the death knell of the country's extensive canal system, and, after the Civil War, put roads on the back burner for decades. The nation's roads became an afterthought for government, business, and citizens in general.

Long before trains, and even before the canal digging boom of the 1820s and 1830s, the federal government had once ventured into the interstate road-building business. It wasn't an altogether smooth or successful attempt, through no fault of the early Congress that recognized the need for overland transportation. But it set the country on a century-long course that we would eventually regret.

The first major entry into the realm of public roads was for what initially was called the Cumberland Road, which later became known as the National Road, planned to link Baltimore and St. Louis. Although President Thomas Jefferson signed legislation in 1806 authorizing construction and funding for the road, building didn't begin until 1811 and didn't reach the western terminus of Vandalia, Illinois, until 1841. The road never did get as far as St. Louis. Construction was stymied by contractor fraud, poor workmanship, and difficulties inherent in working in wilderness areas, where it was difficult to obtain equipment and road-building materials.

One of the most serious problems didn't involve practical or logistical concerns; it was political. Because a strong states' rights attitude prevailed at the time and the federal government was weak, many states opposed spending government money on something that they thought would benefit only some citizens and certain portions of the country. The political opposition went beyond regional rivalries and raised the fundamental question of the federal government's role in such things. The road stirred passionate feelings among those who felt that the federal government had neither the legal right nor the duty to pay for or build roads. By wanting to build a road connecting the nation's new capital with its vast holdings west of the mountains, the early Congress unwittingly established a political philosophy for internal improvements that prevailed until the second decade of the twentieth century.

President Monroe once vetoed an annual appropriations bill that would have provided continued funding for construction of the National Road, arguing that such activity was in direct violation of the country's constitution. Internal improvements were the responsibility of state and local governments, not the federal level, Monroe and others claimed. Though federal money for the road continued for several more years before being ended, this lesser known "Monroe doctrine" helped establish the federal government's non-involvement in infrastructure projects for many decades.

That public works, including roads, contradicted the frontier spirit of America in the 19th century was perhaps perfectly exemplified in Billings County, Dakota Territory. Newly elected county supervisors passed an ordinance in 1886 promising "to hang, burn, or drown any man that will ask for public improvements at the expense of the county."

For at least two generations, roads were left up to local officials and residents to debate, fund, and build...if they were built at all. So by the early 1900s, when reality consisted of a new world and technological advances that President Monroe and those Dakota Territory supervisors couldn't have imagined, the condition of the country's road system reflected those 19th century attitudes. Outside city limits, counties or townships and often farmers themselves maintained market roads, for better or worse. Townships routinely paid local farmers to drag roads near their farms to try to level the inevitable ruts and fill in the mud holes.

A decade into the 20th century, the nation was just beginning to emerge from the dark ages of road building. U.S. Department of Transportation records indicate that, in 1912, the country had approximately 2,199,600 miles of rural roads and only 190,476 miles (8.66 percent of the total) had improved surfaces of gravel, stone, sand-clay, brick, shells, oiled earth, or bituminous material. Keep in mind that, while more than two million miles of roads sounds very impressive, the majority of those miles were two-track trails, not what we would consider a road in the 21st century.

Between 1911 and 1920 powerful road backers surged into action to map out long distance, even transcontinental, routes. However, these early attempts were simply to connect already existing dirt roads into a continual highway, instead of building new roads. The National Old Trails Road was the earliest example, making use of the National Road and westward expansion wagon train routes such as the Santa Fe Trail.

Other routes—the Lincoln Highway, the Dixie Highway, the Jefferson Highway, the Pikes Peak Ocean to Ocean Highway and several more—followed in rapid succession. These roads resulted from private sector leadership, with help from local communities and industry, not from an overarching national scheme of any kind. For good reason, highway historians refer to the years between 1910 and 1925 as the "Named Highways" era.

Dedication of these roads did not mean immediate new construction. They simply linked existing roads and trails together on a map. Because naming a highway didn't really change things on the ground (road signs and improvements to the road itself were many months or even years in the future) this phenomenon had its share of critics. Wags called the Lincoln Highway "an imaginary line on the map" and "a line connecting all the worst mud holes in the country".

In her 1911 book Mrs. Fisher described driving in Wyoming on the trail that, just two years later, would become part of the Lincoln Highway:

> "The road was sandy, with high centres, and the ground squirrels had burrowed into the ground, making it dangerous travelling for motorists. Every now and then we would find ourselves taking a sudden jump as the rear wheels would be buried in these holes."

This passage was simply a matter-of-fact statement, reflecting the reality that those "roads" were nothing more than paths, with no special construction or maintenance to separate them from the adjacent virgin landscape. Mrs. Fisher also made some other interesting observations about travel on rural roads in 1910s America. Describing her trip between Hawthorne and Mina, Nevada, on a two-track trail, she

A typical scene on early 20th century roads. Following rain storms, hard clay turned into deep mud due to lack of improved surfaces and drainage. Car tires further churned the mud into a seemingly bottomless quagmire. (Photo used by permission of the University of Michigan Bentley Library)

wrote, "I am certain there were two thousand whiskey bottles lining the road through which we passed." Near Tonopah, Nevada, she documented seeing "a trail filled with empty tin cans, bottles, glass, etc."

What she saw was the detritus from two generations of travelers on horseback, stagecoach, and covered wagons over those very same trails. The issue of 50 years' worth of trash on these trails was more than just an insult to her aesthetic sensibilities. Given the state of tire and inner tube technology at that time, this debris represented a constant threat of flat tires.

The Lincoln Highway was the first to be named a "highway" per se. This was done for obvious public relations reasons, but it didn't fool many people. Contemporary writers frequently noted that, one day in 1913, the Lincoln Highway was a series of existing unimproved dirt roads and old stagecoach trails, and the next day it was a highway.

Nationally-known writer, world traveler, and later social protocol maven Emily Post spoke for many early travelers when she described her first experience on the highway in her 1916 book *By Motor to the Golden Gate*. She was travelling from New York to San Francisco and the Panama-Pacific Exposition in 1915 with her son—as driver and mechanic—and a friend.

> "Thirty six miles out of Chicago we met the Lincoln Highway and from the first found it a disappointment. As the most important, advertised and lauded road in our country, its first appearance was not engaging. If it were called the cross continent trail you would expect little, but the very word "highway" suggests macadam at the least. And with such titles as 'Transcontinental" and "Lincoln" put before it you dream of a wide straight road…you wake rather unhappily to the actuality of a meandering dirt road that becomes mud half a foot deep after a day or two of rain."

In late 1915 *Collier's Magazine* published three lengthy articles by Miss Post about her transcontinental trip. Given the interest in domestic travel and the "See America First" initiative, the series would have had a large and receptive audience. Indicative of the times, when Post asked a well-traveled friend to recommend the best road to take to San Francisco, the friend, without hesitating a moment, declared "the Union Pacific!" When she pressed her friend further, expressing interest in an automobile route, not a railroad, the friend persisted and simply said that no existing road would get her to California. Post's experienced acquaintance may have been exaggerating a bit, but was closer to the truth than most Americans realized.

Almost certainly, the Van Buren sisters were aware of and likely read these installments since they were also anticipating such a journey the next year. I'm sure that many people who were planning to travel by car or motorcycle read the stories with interest and with an eye toward learning what to do and not to do on a similar trip.

Miss Post was one of many well-to-do Americans who had spent several years traveling the paved roads of Europe before hostilities took over there. She also traveled widely in New York and New England, where road conditions were better than in the remainder of the country. She was accustomed to modern roads, and the reality of travel in rural America came as quite a shock.

CRITICISM ABOUT early long-distance routes, though understandable, was unfair. The American public, institutions, corporations, and governments, were collectively responsible for the abysmal state of the country's roads. The Lincoln Highway Association, with backing from many industrialists and local leaders, had moved aggressively to upgrade the highway, and, by the time Miss Post traveled across it, construction was underway to improve the worst portions and to build bridges across the many streams it traversed. In 1913 bridges over many small streams did not exist. This shortcoming was aggressively attacked, and, within two years, many of these streams were bridged. The Lincoln Highway was finally graveled across its entire length in the mid-1920s. These mostly private sector improvements were taking place on several other interstate routes.

OTHER REALITIES of travel in America a hundred years ago would be unheard of today. From western Nebraska to the California border, early travelers frequently encountered gates that ranchers installed to control cattle. Drivers accepted the responsibility for opening and closing these gates as they motored across grazing lands. Some ranchers actually constructed fences across roads, requiring drivers to detour until they could find passage again.

Farmers and ranchers sometimes took advantage of the situation to bolster their mostly meager incomes. It was common for farmers to provide wrecker service at a time when teams of horses were the only means to extract cars hopelessly stuck in the mud. Sometimes they were especially inventive and imaginative. A 1916 *Chicago Sunday Tribune* article advised: "Avoid Mudhole and Save Money." The paper warned motorists driving from Milwaukee to Chicago:

"Be on lookout for a mud hole three miles west of Evanston. A trench crosses the road, appearing manmade. It is claimed that a nearby farmer has made $500 dragging cars out of the hole at $5–10 per haul."

A *New York Times* article described a similar act of intentional sabotage on a road that ensnared world traveler Harriet White Fisher near her New Jersey home in 1912. Fisher described how she became trapped in a large manmade mud hole on the main road between Trenton and Lakewood. A group of men, who had been loitering nearby with shovels in hand, approached her car and, in a decidedly unfriendly manner, told her that they could either dig her out or she could remain stuck. They bragged that they had "saved" at least four other cars from the same hole, which had the suspicious appearance of having been dug by hand because as it was the only place along the entire length of road that wasn't smooth and dry.

A SITUATION THAT created much frustration for travelers was their difficulty identifying what road they were on. Until then only neighboring residents had been using local roads, and they didn't need road signs. Once long distance travelers began using them, it became necessary to know which roads went where. Travelers around 1913 had to stop frequently to ask directions. Since most farmers rarely knew the road system beyond their local area, drivers had to stop every ten or twenty miles to ensure that they were on the right road.

To address this problem, various publishers began printing very detailed maps giving explicit directions, such as telling a driver to "go 1.3 miles beyond the creek and then turn right at the white barn on the north side of the road." Roads such as the Lincoln Highway and others began being signed with distinctive markings on telephone or telegraph poles, but these were hit and miss. What might be considered adequate signing did not appear for several more years. All in all, traveling even the nation's best known highways in the pre-World War I era was always an uncertain adventure.

FOLLOWING SEVERAL decades with no role, the federal government played a very limited part in roads beginning in 1905, the same year

Henry B. Joy, president of the Packard Motor Car Company, confers with other drivers in a convoy he was leading across the country on the muddy Lincoln Highway in 1915. (Photo used by permission of the University of Michigan / Bentley Library)

the U.S. Forest Service was established. Several offices in the U.S. Department of Agriculture were consolidated into the Office of Public Roads. Staff in this agency provided advisory guidance to other federal agencies regarding road building on federal lands, especially national woodlands.

In 1912 Congress also appropriated funds for the improvement of Post Roads, in conjunction with states and interested local governments that were required to provide matching funds. The U.S. Department of Transportation cites this concept as the forerunner of the subsequent federal highway construction aid program.

In 1916 the federal government bravely waded into the treacherous waters of road construction. The tip-toe "baby steps" taken in the preceding few years had opened the door, and public sentiment had clearly changed from opposing to supporting a federal role. A 1915 editorial in the *Terre Haute Star* showed a change in attitude. Titled "People Must Pull Together for Government Road Aid," it said in part:

"Public sentiment throughout the United States is overwhelmingly in favor of federal aid in highway improvement, as shown in the report recently made to Congress by the joint committee on federal aid. It is no longer the question of the desirability of a national law providing for such governmental help in creating a national system of good roads nor of the constitutionality of such an act, but of deciding upon a measure whose provisions shall be so carefully framed that when enacted into law it will be so equitable and effective that it will remain practically unchanged for many years and will be a credit to the Congress that enacts it."

Roy D. Chapin, an industrialist from Detroit who would later become involved in the automobile industry and serve as President Hoover's Secretary of Commerce, was one of many influential leaders who wrote essays about the See America First concept. He and others had much to gain from this economic force that we now call tourism. He was also a leading proponent and active advocate for the Lincoln Highway and a Pan American Highway, linking the North and South American continents.

Chapin wrote an article in 1915, published in papers across the nation, with the headline: "America for American Motorists." He went to great lengths to extol the beauty of America, favorably comparing this country's natural and manmade attractions with the best of Europe's. One of his essays ended thusly, "These and countless other wonders of man and nature await the eye of the tourist who has not, but should, See America First."

To say the least, Mr. Chapin was being optimistic when describing the American road system of 1915. He surely would have been aware of a trip that Detroit industrial cohort and friend Henry Joy was taking on the Lincoln Highway at that very time. Joy was President of the Packard Automobile Company and was one of the most outspoken cheerleaders for the automobile and travel industries in America. He was also a major supporter of the Lincoln Highway, lending his name and giving his money to the project. He personally made several trips across the road in Packard automobiles, ostensibly for testing and advertising purposes, though he was also an active outdoors person who loved the challenge of the trip.

JOY AVOIDED CITIES and hotels, preferring instead to sleep on the ground and rough it to the degree possible, much to the chagrin of company staff who had to accompany him on such trips. At the same time that Mr. Chapin's article was likely making quite an impression on readers, Mr. Joy was spending endless days pushing his Packard out of the muddy ruts that characterized America's roads that summer. It had been unusually rainy in the Midwest in 1915, and it took Joy eleven days to drive the approximately 1,000 miles from Chicago to Cheyenne because of the extremely muddy conditions that stretched across Illinois, Iowa, and Nebraska.

Automobile manufacturers, the Good Roads organization, the American Automobile Association, and many governmental entities jumped on the domestic tourism bandwagon, and the See America First campaign gathered momentum. The opportunity for Americans to consider traveling around their country solely for recreation, an unheard of notion just a few years earlier, had finally arrived.

A critical mass of support had developed, and it had finally become clear that the roads needed to connect all parts of the country in a cohesive and useful system must have oversight and planning at a national level. Congress passed the Federal Aid Road Act of 1916, providing a funding assistance program to states to build roads. This financial aid program had just begun to show results in 1917 when the country's entry into World War I once again put road construction and maintenance on the back burner.

After the war, federal attention was finally directed toward the sorry state of the nation's roads. The picture had become even clearer because of the war. The Army found that it could not adequately move men and materials on existing roads, and that railroads alone were inadequate to meet the demands of national defense.

A 1919 event ultimately greatly affected how Americans would travel in the future and also changed the life of young Army Captain Dwight D. Eisenhower, who was involved in the U.S. Army's Cross

Country Motor Transport Train. This multi-faceted effort sent a convoy of 80 of the latest military vehicles across the country to test them in real world conditions, to serve public relations purposes, and to ascertain the nation's ability to respond to another national crisis by conducting a realistic movement of men and materiel across the continent.

The departing ceremony took place July 9 on the Ellipse in front of the White House. The convoy left Washington and traveled north to Gettysburg, Pennsylvania. The vehicles got on the Lincoln Highway there, following it all the way across the country to San Francisco. Despite the fact that the Lincoln Highway was one of the most famous and frequently used roads in America, one of the most important people in that Army convoy was a scout who drove ahead each day to find the road and mark it so that the military vehicles wouldn't get lost.

However, following the Lincoln Highway's route was only one problem; staying on it was another. Vehicles slipped off the roads into ditches and regularly got stuck in deep mud and sand. The soldiers on the convoy had to push, pull, curse, and otherwise maneuver heavy trucks to free them from the clutches of miles of mud. Many bridges were just barely able to carry cars, and the heavy military vehicles crashed through them. The Army had to strengthen bridges or build new ones at some locations. In some cases, the only option was to ford the rivers and creeks.

On a trip of more than 3,000 miles, the Army expected some problems, but the reality was much worse. The bad roads damaged tires, axles, motors, and anything that could be shaken off or cracked as the vehicles traversed the rough road. The humbled convoy didn't arrive in San Francisco until September 5, broken and tired. Captain Eisenhower and the entire military establishment were shocked to see the abysmally poor road conditions, and this realization helped shape policy for decades to come.

Nearly forty years later, in 1956, President Eisenhower created the Interstate Highway System. It is a common belief that seeing the German Autobahn during World War II led Eisenhower to create the Interstate Highway system. However, equally significant was the very difficult trip across his own country as a young officer (twenty-five years before being appointed as the Supreme Commander of Allied forces in Europe) that convinced him of the need for a highway network that would serve all of the country's needs—economic, tourism, travel, and national defense. It's interesting to note that Captain Eisenhower had seriously considered quitting the military in 1919 before he took part in the cross country convoy. That trip not only helped change America, it also changed his future plans. And the rest is history.

Partially as a result of the military's cross-country convoy experience, the Federal Aid Highway Act of 1921 became a critical piece of legislation that forever changed how America's roads would be designed, built, paid for, and located. Congress created the Bureau of Public Roads, which commissioned General John J. Pershing to draw up a blueprint for a road system to ensure national defense. The General drafted what became known as the Pershing Map, with recommended routes for roads across America. Eventually, virtually all of his proposed roads were constructed, and we can thank General Pershing for the look of today's American highway map.

Soon, named roads were relegated to the annals of history, replaced with logically numbered highways. Thus the Lincoln Highway became U.S. 30, the National Road became U.S. 40, and the Trail to Sunset became U.S. 66. Routes were well marked and permanent, so local units of government could no longer decide the path of interstate roads and could no longer change them on a whim.

By the First World War, America had a well established automobile manufacturing industry and was beginning to address the complex issue of roads. But one more indispensible component of the three-legged economic behemoth created by motor vehicles had to be addressed. That final critical ingredient for an economy based on a motorized transportation system was fuel, and such a system must have a dependable supply of it. Enter the final industrial component of the early 20th century economy—oil companies.

Americans had a love/hate relationship with the nation's suppliers of crude oil and gasoline in the 1910s much as we do today. Unexplained fluctuations in the price of a gallon of gasoline mystified buyers then as they do now. The year 1915 saw such a dramatic increase in gasoline prices that the U.S. Federal Trade Commission investigated the matter and published an exhaustive tome: *Report of the Price of Gasoline* in 1915. Congress had created the commission just one year earlier in an attempt to prevent monopolies and ensure fair competition.

The commission prepared its report when competition among dozens of producers and refineries was fierce and shortly after the breakup of Standard Oil Company's near monopolistic hold on the industry. The FTC noted that the amount of gasoline consumed had increased dramatically in 1915, up 38 percent from the prior year, and an astonishing 74 percent more than just two years earlier. The report documented considerable disparity in gasoline costs by state, much like today.

In the earliest days, gasoline was sold in limited quantities in hardware stores and pharmacies. As the demand for a dependable supply of gasoline rose, repair garages began offering it, and ultimately gas stations appeared on the scene.

Increases in the cost of gasoline experienced in 1915 were only the beginning of a long upward trend, as demand for petroleum products steadily climbed in civilian as well as military markets in subsequent years. By early 1917 gasoline had hit the unheard of level of 33 cents per gallon in much of the country (more than double the cost in 1915), and continued its upward trend to nearly 40 cents that summer. Forty-cents-per-gallon gasoline in 1917 terms equates to a shocking $7.45 per gallon in 2011 dollars!

The FTC's nearly 300-page report detailed the crude oil, refinery, pipeline, and gasoline situation of a century ago. Change the dates and amounts, and it could have been published much more recently. The commission identified not just one cause for the dramatic increases in 1915 gasoline prices, but attributed it to myriad complex reasons.

The 1915 FTC report did strongly recommend that gasoline quality be addressed. The Commission reported that laboratory tests showed a steady decline in the quality of gasoline during 1914 and 1915. However, it also noted that no specific standard existed for the many chemical constituents of gasoline, so it was impossible to point

It was not until the 1920s that gas stations such as this were even somewhat commonplace along America's roads. During the first two decades of the last century gasoline was purchased at a variety of places, including hardware stores, motorcycle and automobile dealers, repair garages, and general stores. (Photo by author)

fingers of blame. Report authors recommended tightening the standards for what was called gasoline, but admitted that it would be a daunting task because dozens of manufacturers were building engines with very different fuel needs. Gasoline supply and quality issues affected every driver then and continue to be important elements in fueling the nation's passion for automobiles.

America's Love Affair
With Motorcycles

—◦◦◦—

When I go to heaven / Harley Harley heaven / I want to meet a King /
Like the Panhead 48 / I want to meet the Fat One /
We can talk for hours / When my time has come, Babe /
I won't be running late.
Flying high / Riders in the sky / Na na na na.
When I go to heaven / Red-skin heaven / I want to meet the Chiefs /
Yea, I want to meet all Scouts /
I won't miss my friends cos I know where they'll be /
We're all part of the Indian Family.[1]

Like everything connected to motorized vehicles circa 1900, motorcycles also had a gradual beginning and evolved over a decade to what became known and accepted as "motorcycles" in people's minds and recognized as such in the law. Learning about the development of bicycles can help us truly appreciate the history of motorcycles. The modern bicycle, with its chain-driven rear wheel, came into common use in the 1880s. With this major leap forward in technology and safety, bicycling became a very popular pastime in the 1880s and 1890s, bringing people of all ages and genders out to ride park avenues and city streets.

One development that no one predicted was the bicycle's role in women's efforts to break from the constraints of Victorian Era behav-

---

[1] Lyrics by Roxetter © JimmyFun Music 1994

ioral limitations. The social trend-setters of the day raised few objections to women riding two-wheelers, and in fact encouraged it as a healthy form of exercise and recreation. Many women viewed the activity in much more meaningful terms than simple recreation, however. Bicycles became a means to breach the barriers restricting women.

Susan B. Anthony, a leader in the suffrage and women's rights movements, put it this way:

> "Let me tell you what I think of bicycling. I think it has done more to emancipate women than anything else in the world. It gives women a feeling of freedom and self-reliance. I stand and rejoice every time I see a woman ride by on a wheel...the picture of free, untrammeled womanhood."

This might seem an exaggerated emotional response today, but realizing the context in which the sentiments were expressed makes it easier to appreciate the role that the humble bicycle played in society.

PREDICTABLY, SOMEBODY soon tried to fit a motor on a bicycle frame to create the first powered bicycle. Gottlieb Daimler is credited with building what is considered the first motorcycle in 1885, though they were not called that for many more years. It was a crude machine with wooden wheels and frame, powered by a single cylinder "Otto-cycle" engine, but it got the wheels turning and the evolutionary process took over.

In the 1890s several European manufacturers produced motorized two-wheelers, and Massachusetts-based Metz Company built what is considered America's first motorized bicycle—a model they called the Orient-Aster—in 1898. Charles Metz was credited with coining the word "motorcycle" in 1900 at a Boston race where one of their early motorized bikes was competing. In 1905 Metz merged with David Marsh—another Massachusetts builder of motorized bicycles—and they formed the American Motorcycle Company. The Marsh-Metz motorcycle—universally called the MM—was its first model.

Many early models of "motorcycles" were simply bicycles with small motors attached. They even had the usual pedal and chain mechanism so that it could be pedaled like a bicycle if the motor failed. Bicycle

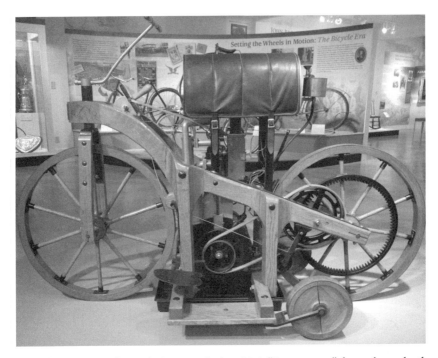

Several versions of Gottlieb Daimler's 1885 "Reitwagen" have been built. Daimler's original version was the first two-wheeled vehicle to have a four-stroke gasoline engine installed. He built his original machine primarily as a test vehicle for research purposes. (photo by author)

shops began to sell both plain and motorized bicycles. Bicycling journals also began to cater their coverage to the many riders who were enthusiastically moving on to the new motorized two-wheelers.

In many ways, enthusiasts made a seamless transition from bicycling to motorcycling. After the turn of the century, motorcycles began evolving to the point that they could be truly considered as a distinct vehicle, not simply a modified bicycle, and gradually the connection between bicycle and motor-cycle dissolved.

In 1901 Hendee Manufacturing Company of Springfield, Massachusetts, produced the first ground-up American motorcycle later called the Indian. The "Indian" model name was a carryover from the 1890s when Hendee Manufacturing made the Indian bicycle. In 1903 William S. Harley and Arthur Davidson of Milwaukee built a motorcycle in a 10' x 15' wooden shed with the name Harley-Davidson Motor Company hand-painted on the door. Walter Davidson joined the effort later that year, and in 1907 William Davidson quit his day job with the railroad and became part of the new Harley-Davidson Motor Company. Once the floodgates opened, many companies clambered to make motorcycles, and the technology—and thus power, speed, comfort, and reliability—improved rapidly. For over a decade in the early 20th century the motorcycle became the preferred means of transportation for the masses.

It was around 1903 that people began to consider motorized bicycles as a completely different vehicle than human-powered bicycles. On September 7th of that year, enthusiasts and industry leaders, including George Hendee of Hendee Manufacturing Company, formed the Federation of American Motorcyclists (FAM).

The FAM was actually a group that broke away from the National Cycling Association—the organization that sanctioned bicycle races and lobbied on behalf of the rights and interests of non-motorized cycle riders. Those who rode motorized bicycles became numerous enough, and the machines they rode distinct enough from common bicycles, to warrant the recognition of a new class of vehicle and operator and an entity to lobby on their behalf. A new sanctioning body was also needed to oversee the many events and races with motorized bicycles and early motorcycles. The FAM became that organization.

The role of the FAM was clearly delineated in its constitution, which read in part:

> "Its objects shall be to encourage the use of motorcycles and to promote the general interests of motorcycling; to ascertain, defend and protect the rights of motorcyclists; to facilitate touring; to assist in the good roads movement, and to advise and assist in the regulation of motorcycle racing and other competition in which motorcycles engage."

These fundamental operating principles have endured remarkably unchanged over the decades, and most of these priorities continue to be those of the current American Motorcyclist Association, which can trace its roots to the FAM.

ANOTHER FACTOR in the evolution of the motorcycle involved the legal system and governmental regulations. For several years the legal status of motorized two-wheelers was unclear. Were these contraptions technically bicycles, and thus outside of the new regulations involving licensing, or were they more akin to automobiles, and thus required to follow the various new traffic and licensing requirements. The FAM certainly didn't help clarify matters. In its first six years it actually fought to have motorcycles considered as bicycles in the eyes of the ever-broadening statutes regulating motorized vehicles.

Mr. Earle Ovington, writing in the April 1909 edition of *Motor Cycle Illustrated*, stated what most riders may have felt at the time, "The motorcycle is essentially a bicycle, except, instead of being propelled by the muscular energy of the rider, it is driven by a small gasoline engine."

Indeed, the earliest motorized two-wheelers seemed to be more bicycle than motor vehicle. The frames had been beefed up a bit to handle the additional weight and engine torque. The wheels and tires were just a bit larger and heavier duty, and engine controls were added. However, the vehicle still had a bicycle look and feel in those days.

The federation was at least partially successful in its arguments that these modified bicycles should not be treated the same as automobiles. The state of New York legally defined motorcycles as bicycles and exempted them from registration requirements through 1910.

Elsewhere, confusion was the order of the day. For example, in the City of Detroit the county prosecutor filed a legal action in 1908, attempting to clarify the legal status of motorcycles. In a fascinating twist, the defendant was both a Detroit police officer and the president of the Detroit Motorcycle Club. The prosecutor brought the charges against patrolman H.G. Smith to force the court to issue an opinion as to whether or not a motorcycle was legally a motor vehicle and subject to the same licensing and traffic control regulations that applied to automobiles. In deference to Officer Smith's position, the prosecutor allowed him to voluntarily appear in court to answer the charges. This matter was made more interesting by the fact that Smith's wife was also an active motorcyclist.

Judges came down on the side of licensing authorities, and the questions of whether motorcycles had to be licensed, and were bound by traffic regulations, were quickly answered.

IT IS CLEAR from the zealous feelings and attitudes expressed by enthusiasts in trade journals of a century ago that early riders were as unabashedly fervent in the pleasure they derived from their sport as bikers are today. Riders then wrote passionately about the joys of the open road. They tried to explain the physical and visceral feelings they experienced when riding a powered two-wheeled vehicle and wrote of the social and community aspects of riding and of club membership. They exhibited the pride that came with ownership of a particular brand and, then as now, they were somewhat smug about being part of a small group that had its own rules and behaviors.

Flipping the pages of old magazines provides a picture of enthusiasts who loved to travel and enjoyed regaling others with the details of their adventures…the good and the bad. Riders unquestionably gained a certain amount of "macho" credit by enduring terrible road conditions, cold or wet weather, and mechanical breakdowns. Their experiences, told and retold, converted into stories of high adventure and great fun through a mysterious story-telling alchemy that continues to this day.

The motorcycling community then, as now, was a mix of personalities. A hundred years ago, it was as common to find a Yale or Harvard upperclassman taking a ride dressed in his best attire as it was to see a blue collar rider in well-worn work clothes. It was impossible then to describe who a typical rider was or to find consensus as to why they rode, just as it is today. Bikers rode motorcycles in the early 20th century for the same complex reasons that they ride in the early 21st century. If riders who have a quarter million miles under their belts are asked why they ride, they will struggle for a rational answer.

To the core of their being riders know exactly why they lust for the feel, sound, motion, and look of a motorcycle, but they will have difficulty articulating those emotions to another. To read the articles and letters in motorcycling journals of four generations ago is strikingly similar to reading a current magazine. The early writings also spoke of brand loyalty, comfort, and reliability of the machine. They, too, wrote of enjoyable trips and destinations, the sublime delight of cruising down a scenic road with the wind in your hair and the sun in your face, and the pleasures of camaraderie with others who shared the passion for the sport. They had similar complaints about rules and regulations…and the burden of having to endure too many…and the condition of roads. They also were concerned about the future of motorcycling. A publisher from either era could quite easily adapt to the opposite end of the time spectrum.

PRIDE IN ownership and the longing to leave one's own imprint has also existed for as long as motorcycles have. Early journals carried numerous technical articles about do-it-yourself maintenance. They ranged from necessary basics such as performing on-the-road tire and tube repairs, to technically demanding projects such as grinding valves and re-enameling metal surfaces. The practice of customizing motorcycles to make them one's own commenced immediately after mass production began, and articles discussed this growing phenomenon. This activity has certainly grown more popular with time.

It did not take long for motorcycle travel to mature beyond the concept of simply taking a ride. A 1917 *Motor Cycle Illustrated* article titled "A College Course on Wheels" discussed a concept that many motorcyclists today can readily relate to—the educational benefits of motorcycling if one explores and rides with a focus on discovery. The sub-heading of the article went on to state: "What the motorcycle rider who travels with his eyes open can acquire in the way of education through use of the two-wheeler." The author then wrote simply and convincingly of how riders can learn about history, geography, physics, law, and art by exploring the world around them with a sense of wonder and curiosity. The author also expounded on the value of the mechanical knowledge one obtained from operating and repairing a machine, which had application in all areas of their lives.

Articles in many magazines and newspapers described in the most positive manner the many practical ways that businesses and governmental agencies were making use of these remarkably utilitarian vehicles. One such story, published in the *Boston Daily Globe* in 1915, enthusiastically extolled the value of these machines in virtually every sector of American society. When you consider that the machines had an even greater following in the recreational and competitive arenas, it is easy to understand the enthusiasm for motorcycles in that era.

The headline declared "Motorcycle Has Variety of Uses" and went on to explain some of those novel applications. The article read:

> "Hundreds of daily demonstrations are proof of the utility, speed, and economy of the modern motorcycle. There is scarcely a field of activity that the two-wheeler has not entered and proven its value.
>
> "The motorcycle enables the physician to reach its patient in less time than ever before, making it possible to eliminate many hours of human suffering. The motorcycle is a part of every progressive police department, carrying mounted officers to the scene of crime or accidents and enabling them to run down violators of the law. The motorcycle aids the forest ranger in protecting our great timber lands from fire. The motorcycle carries mail and delivers telegrams.
>
> "The motorcycle rushes the important prescription to the bedside of the suffering. The motorcycle hurries the pulmotor [a resuscitation device] to the beach where every second counts in the effort to restore life. A motorcycle mounted guard accompanies the President of the United States on his trips about the capital.
>
> "Uses of the motorcycle in the Army are almost unlimited. Motorcycle dispatch riders and scouts have won great fame for themselves in the present European struggle. Machine guns mounted on motorcycles are carried to their positions on the battlefield; motorcycles with sidecars hurry supplies to the Red Cross workers who are seeking to relieve the injured soldiers in the hospitals."

The newspaper story continued at length detailing the many and varied virtues and uses of these marvelous new machines. And they didn't overlook the fact that many motorcyclists rode purely for pleasure. The article went on to say:

"The ease with which the two-wheeler is operated, its reliability and comfort, make it an ideal vehicle for touring. Club sociability and endurance runs are enjoyed by thousands of riders all over the country. More and more we hear of the long-distance tourist, riding from ocean to ocean, from gulf to lakes, around the United States or circling the globe, for pleasure. Many of these long-distance tourists are women, who find as much pleasure in the sport as do the men."

All in all, quite an endorsement for this new mode of transportation that was sweeping the nation. Economy of operation was also a benefit. They cost less than cars and many models got well over fifty miles per gallon (mpg), with some of the lightweight models getting close to one hundred mpg. Sheriff Ben Bradenburg of Dallas County, Texas, declared in a 1915 article in the *Indianapolis Star*, "One motorcycle will do the work of three mounted men and does not cost as much as one horse."

In America's heartland, a businessman in Waterloo, Iowa, who sold Indian brand motorcycles, understood the financial rewards that he could realize by convincing farmers that a switch from horses to motorcycles made perfect sense. To tap into this seemingly unlikely market, the Guy W. Campbell Agency advertised motorcycles as a solution to the inherent loneliness and isolation that characterized life in rural America a century ago.

His 1915 advertisement in the *Waterloo Evening Courier* made it seem that the old ways could be changed overnight simply by buying one of his Indian motorcycles. The ad header proclaimed, "Move Your Farm Nearer Town" and, with logic that was hard to argue, the ad continued:

"Wouldn't you go to town oftener—not alone for business, but for enjoyment too—if it didn't take so long to make the trip by horse and buggy? Thousands of farmers are doing it, keeping in touch with what's going on, and enjoying every foot of the way by riding an Indian Motorcycle."

A significant difference between then and today is that a great many motorcycle owners rode their machines year-round. Early magazines have scores of pictures showing recreational riders, and working people such as linemen and letter carriers, riding their motorcycles, often with sidecars, in below-freezing temperatures and through deep snow. Today, only a tiny minority of owners ride in the winter.

Sidecars enjoyed a brief period of widespread use in the early 20th century. Motorcycle owners wanted the capability of carrying a passenger safely and comfortably, while workers needed a place to carry items. Various mechanical devices were developed to accomplish this—small trailers, "rear cars" and "fore cars", which, as the names suggest, attached to either end of a motorcycle.

Passengers in trailers and rear cars were subjected to the noise and smoke of the machine, as well as being struck by rocks, mud, and other road debris. The fore car had its own pitfalls, including making it difficult for operators to maneuver the machine and to see where they were going.

In 1903 England's Graham brothers decided to try a new approach: remove one of the wheels from a trailer and attach it directly to the side of a motorcycle. Thus the side car was born. This development allowed a passenger to ride in relative comfort and safety, while also providing a place for workers who used motorcycles on the job to carry tools and equipment.

Sidecars today look remarkably similar to models of many years ago. Today they're ABS plastic or fiberglass and have better suspension, lights, and such, but their basic appearance is quite similar, and they enjoy a small but passionate following.

ONE MUST constantly hearken back to what was considered normal a century ago to keep things in proper perspective. Up to that time people expected to be exposed to the elements when they had to travel from one place to another other than by train. Whether going in the family buggy pulled by a horse, riding on horseback, or walking, those who lived in that era had always known that going somewhere for whatever reason, or working out of doors, meant being exposed to and affected by existing weather conditions. Even early cars lacked all but the most rudimentary protection from the weather, and no shelter at all from the ambient temperature.

Travel by motorcycle thus added no additional discomfort than typical horse-powered travel, but had the distinct advantage of being quicker and easier and, owners would argue, more enjoyable. Additionally, they didn't have to harness a team of horses to prepare for a trip, and didn't have to care for them after completing the outing; they could simply park the motorcycle.

In any event, exchanging a horse of flesh and blood for one made of iron was an easy adjustment to make, and in the pre-war period motorcycles became very popular. Today, many Americans may consider the motorcycle as a primarily recreational vehicle, albeit with practical transportation uses as well, but back then many saw them as work vehicles that made their lives easier and their work more efficient.

Even today, farmers in places such as Afghanistan carry their entire family on their motorcycle for a trip into town, while millions of city dwellers in Asia depend on the inexpensive and fuel-efficient two-wheeler as their main form of transportation, not as recreational vehicles.

After 1920, when automobiles became fully enclosed and offered greater protection from the elements, the use of motorcycles as utilitarian vehicles dropped rapidly, and they largely became a machine for enthusiasts, much like today.

WITH THE explosion in motorcycles' popularity in the early 1900s, many companies got into the manufacturing fray—dozens in the United States alone, in addition to scores overseas. The competition was fierce and innovations progressed rapidly, making a 1915 model motorcycle significantly more dependable, comfortable, and powerful than one built just a few years earlier.

In 1913 Hendee Manufacturing was the world's largest motorcycle manufacturer, producing an astounding 32,000 units that year. The U.S. Army unwittingly played a major role in deciding which manufacturers would survive this turbulent period when they named Hendee and Harley-Davidson models as the standard motorcycles for the Army Motor Transport Division, along with (to many people's surprise) the Solo brand made by British manufacturer Bradbury.

Mexican Pancho Villa's attacks on American soil provided the American Army with an excellent opportunity to test motorcycles in warfare. General Pershing's options for moving men and equipment included cars and motorcycles, as well as traditional mules and horses. The Army had purchased a few Harley-Davidson and Indian machines and outfitted them with sidecars and even machine guns to test in actual combat conditions. Lessons learned from the Mexican experience, already proved in Europe, were that motorcycles were excellent replacements for horses used by dispatch riders, but not so good for moving foot soldiers, nor as a firm stance from which to shoot, at least not with any acceptable level of accuracy.

The First World War had a dramatic effect on the motorcycle manufacturing sector throughout the world. It was a significant, though temporary, boon to American companies, but brought economic decline to their European counterparts. Great Britain declared war on Germany in August 1914 and was able to export nearly 21,000 motorcycles that year, despite being on a war footing for nearly five months. However, once the war was fully underway, that number fell by nearly 50 percent in 1915 and dropped virtually to zero by 1916.

On this side of the Atlantic, a 1917 advertisement by Harley-Davidson boasted, "Sales of Harley-Davidson machines in Latin America this year show an increase of 146 percent over a year ago." Hendee Manufacturing also reported selling significantly more Indian brand motorcycles abroad in 1916. American manufacturers found themselves in the unlikely position of producing machines for Europe, as well as filling the void in other world markets.

The military forces of warring nations became the primary market for motorcycles. In 1918 *Popular Science* magazine reported that the warring nations had used 750,000 motorcycles since hostilities began. The British reportedly had at least 40,000 machines in service by 1915, and the various powers in the Battle of the Marne alone used an estimated 18,000 motorcycles. Manufacturers were running at high capacity to meet the demand, but this increase was double-edged. While the temporary market created by the war resulted in a short-term spike in production, the number of civilians in Europe and the British Commonwealth buying bikes dropped considerably.

This same phenomenon became obvious in the United States when it entered the war in 1917 and 1918. A significant portion of the motorcycle-buying population had been drafted into military service.

Many were killed, and a large portion of returning veterans bore physical or psychological wounds. As a result, the number of motorcyclists declined; a development that wouldn't change for three decades.

In the World War I era several other factors arose that worked against the motorcycle remaining as the vehicle of choice for a large segment of the population. After Henry Ford perfected the moving assembly line in 1914, the price tag of the Ford Model T dropped significantly, actually falling below the level of the latest model motorcycles by the early 1920s. The cost advantages of owning a two-wheeler evaporated and people turned to the practical advantages of owning a four-wheeled vehicle. The Model T quickly became the most popular car in America, and motorcycles became a vehicle appreciated primarily by passionate riders who saw much more than mere practicalities in their machines. Motorcycle manufacturers began disappearing as quickly as they had appeared on the scene less than two decades earlier.

According to the *Wall Street Journal*, in 1923 the Hendee Manufacturing board of directors changed the company's name to Indian Motocycle Company (purposely dropping the "r" from the word motorcycle, following an earlier practice), after several years of management and financial difficulties. Many sources incorrectly cite 1928 as the year the name change occurred. Only Harley-Davidson and Indian survived the Depression of the 1930s. The original Indian Company went bankrupt in 1953, leaving Harley-Davidson as the only major American manufacturer for many years.

Today, Polaris Industries also manufactures the Victory brand of motorcycles, at a plant in Iowa. In April 2011, Polaris acquired the Indian brand from Indian Motorcycle Limited. The Indian marquee has experienced sparks of life in recent decades in several iterations. With the engineering and sales power of Polaris Industries, the Indian brand may yet survive, at least as a limited production or custom motorcycle. Several small American companies also manufacture motorcycles for niche customers who are willing to pay a premium for bragging rights for custom-made motorcycles.

AN INCOMPLETE list of American motorcycle manufacturers circa 1910 includes the following companies: Apache, Armac, American Motor, American Royal, California Racer, Cleveland, Consolidated,

The passion that owners of Indian and Harley-Davidson motorcycles felt for their chosen brand was genuine and ran deep. Arguments were heated and emotions ran high as these two companies competed both on the race track and the sales floor. (Photo by author)

Crest, Curtiss, Cyclone, Dayton, Emblem, Excelsior, Feilbach, Flanders, Flying Merkel, Geer, Greyhound, Harley-Davidson, Hendee, Henderson, Hilaman, Holley, Hornecker, Imperial, Iver-Johnson, Jefferson, Keller & Risque, Marsh-Metz, M.C. Company, Magnet, Marathon, Marvel, Miami, Minneapolis, Monarch, Morgan, N.S.U., New Era, Ovington, Pierce, Pope, Raycycle, Reading-Standard, Reliance, Royal, S-D Manufacturing (had a shaft drive cycle in 1909), Sears, Shaw, Simplex, Steffey, Sylvester-Jones, Thiem, Thomas, Thor, Torpedo, Tourist, Vindec, Wagner, Warwick, Whipple, and Yale.

Victorian Girls Breaking All the Rules

—⟨∾⟩—

By the sea, by the sea, by the beautiful sea!
You and me, you and me, oh how happy we'll be!
When each wave comes a-rolling in
We will duck or swim,
And we'll float and fool around the water.
Over and under, and then up for air,
Pa is rich, Ma is rich, so now what do we care?
I love to be beside your side, beside the sea,
Beside the seaside, by the beautiful sea![1]

A defining characteristic of women travelers and adventurists, who cast off the cloak of comfort and security they could have enjoyed as females, is that they all departed from what was expected of women during this period. Society during the Victorian Era had established certain expectations for women and clearly defined their place. Ironically, although Queen Victoria was the powerful female leader for whom the movement is named, the strictures that comprised the social order of the time made it a man's world, in which males held the power and made the rules.

"Proper" girls of this time, especially in urban America and Great Britain, spent much of their days in "correct" clothing, engaged in pursuits such as sewing, reading, playing the piano, and other genteel pastimes which guaranteed that they would not get dirty, sunburned, or

---

[1] From the musical "For Me and My Gal" by Harold Atteridge and Harry Carroll; 1914

exposed to unsavory persons and behavior. The Van Buren sisters, Effie Hotchkiss, Della Crewe and the several other women presented in this book did not follow the typical pattern for girls of that era. Rather than spend most of their time dressed in the proper clothes and doing the approved activities, these young women were also taught or allowed to ride horses, hunt, camp, canoe, play baseball, climb trees, and do many of the "wrong" things according to the fading Victorian protocols.

It is obvious that they were also poised and confident young women, able to mix with urban intellectuals and high society, as well as enjoy the company of the working class. These women wanted to get their hands dirty, to be physically active and challenged. Expecting to be pampered or protected was not part of their personality.

The record makes it clear that they can thank their fathers for their unorthodox upbringing. The Van Buren sisters, for instance, told reporters that their father insisted on their being exposed to, and trained in, horseback riding, archery, firearms, canoeing, swimming, and more. It is also evident from Effie Hotchkiss's activities as a girl, on the farm and in the city, that she was most certainly not confined to the parlor. Della Crewe, daughter of a carpenter, likewise proved her capacity for hands-on work. She worked at a motorcycle agency where she learned to repair the machines from the bottom up, with no favors shown because she happened to be a woman.

MANY GIRLS AND women were born into situations where a pampered or protected lifestyle simply was not an option and lived their lives outside of Victorian protocols. These niceties didn't extend to most girls born in rural America. Many others shrugged off expectations that kept their society sisters confined, but were not for them. However, even women who resisted restraints imposed on them sometimes yielded to some of those societal pressures.

One of the issues that weighed heavily upon young unmarried women a century ago was their age. Throughout history women had fewer options than men for a variety of reasons. They often had less education and usually lacked the means to be self-supporting because most jobs were not open to them. That meant they needed someone to help support them—either family or a husband. Personal and societal pressures to marry were heavy, and most women expected to be mar-

Alice Ramsey making one of several tire changes on a Maxwell car during her 1909 journey across America. Because her passengers did not know how to drive, Alice piloted the car the entire distance herself, performing her own mechanical repairs. (Public domain photo)

ried by an early age or risk being thought of as spinsters or old maids. Women who fought the system and delayed marriage to pursue their own dreams did so at potentially significant personal cost.

Those societal pressures explain why some women then, including perhaps those of whom I write, misled others about their true age. For whatever reason, the ages reported in newspaper and magazine articles for many subjects of this book were low by several years. This might be a matter of reporters not getting it right, but it may also have been that some of the women deliberately manipulated their age. Regardless of their true age, the stories of these women—free spirits who pursued lifestyles that took them into the world of cars, planes, and motorcycles—are worth writing and reading.

ONE YOUNG WOMAN who did not mind getting her hands dirty or crawling underneath a car to fix it was Alice Huyler Ramsey. She was a graduate of prestigious Vassar College and founder and president of the Women's Motoring Club of New York. Twenty-two year old Alice and three other women left New York City in 1909, bound for the West Coast and driving a Maxwell touring car. Of the foursome, only Alice knew how to drive. She not only drove the entire distance, but also made necessary repairs and changed the many flat tires. Forty-one driving days, 11 tires, and 3,800 miles later, they made history upon arriving in San Francisco, where they were met by much fanfare. Alice had just become the first woman to drive a vehicle completely across the continent.

Curt McConnell provides details of her adventure in *A Reliable Car and a Woman Who Knows It: The First Coast-to-Coast Auto Trips by Women, 1899 – 1916*. He describes the numerous challenges that Alice and her companions experienced during the journey—unimaginably bad roads, frequent flat tires, and various mechanical breakdowns. In the pre-World War I period it was always an adventure, with many possible challenges, when a person went for a drive, whether across the county or across the country. The press noted that Ramsey carried a heavy tow rope, shovel, block and tackle, a tank of compressed air, and long strips of canvas to place under the tires to aid in traction. Cars that ventured out of main cities also routinely carried tire chains to get them through the many muddy stretches.

In 1961 Ramsey chronicled her adventure in a book titled *Veil, Duster and Tire Iron*. On October 17, 2000, Alice Ramsey became the first woman to be inducted into the Automotive Hall of Fame. According to the Hall of Fame citation, "Her courage and determination have inspired countless women to pursue automotive-related goals and dreams."

Ms. Blanche Stuart Scott must have also shocked Victorian purists. She was a precocious and very active Rochester, New York, society girl and "Vassar girl". Her father had given her an automobile when she was just thirteen because he thought that having a car to drive and work on would help keep the gifted, but sometimes difficult, Scott out of trouble, and give her practical skills to use in life. To say he hit the nail on the head is an understatement! She went on to become one of the most famous women in the country—the first to fly an airplane and the second to drive across North America in a car, followed by a very successful career that kept her in the public eye for decades.

It wasn't without some trying times, however. Blanche's presence on the streets of Rochester presented such a danger to the public's health and safety that the city council tried to prevent her from driving. Scott decided to channel her energies and skills in a more focused way. On May 16, 1910, she and a companion left New York City in an Overland car and drove it across the country, then down the west coast to Mexico. But their crossing did not follow the typical approach of previous drivers.

Scott made the trip very much an adventure where point-to-point efficiency was not a concern. Following the Mohawk Valley route across New York, she went around Lake Erie and then dropped down to Columbus, Ohio, to visit Governor Judson Harmon. She then followed the old National Road to Dayton to watch the Wright Brothers do an exhibition flight at the local air field.

Following that, she led a procession of motor enthusiasts into Indianapolis to see the already famous Memorial Day races. The *Elyria Republican* reported that she backtracked all the way from Indianapolis to Toledo to visit the Willys-Overland factory, which manufactured the model that she was driving. After Toledo, she went by way of South Bend to Chicago. Once satisfied that she and her passenger had seen and done all they could in the Windy City, she went north to Milwaukee for a promotional stop, then finally westward once again.

Blanche's trip across the continent was filled with adventures, including a special organ recital for their benefit at the magnificent Mormon Tabernacle in Salt Lake City. Of course, the journey also had its share of trials and tribulations, such as getting stuck in the mud and being lost in the Great Salt Lake Desert for a full day. But make it to California she did, on July 23, whereupon she dumped the traditional bottle of Atlantic Ocean water into the Pacific.

After exploring the state, and making a difficult side trip to the Mexican border, she went to Imperial Beach on August 6 to watch Mr. E. M. Roehrig, a pilot who was making demonstration flights. Persistent and persuasive, Blanche talked her way onto the plane and squeezed next to Roehrig in the tiny cockpit of the Farman biplane. She was ecstatic when he took her aloft for a mile-and-a-half spin and described the flight to a reporter as "the most delightfully exciting experience I ever had."

Once back in New York by way of a train, Scott decided that flying was going to be her future. She talked famed aviator Glenn Curtiss into giving her lessons, but it took a lot of convincing. Curtiss, like most men of the day, did not think a woman possessed the physical strength to handle the manual controls of an early plane, nor was he convinced that women had the emotional force necessary to undertake such a potentially dangerous activity. He also feared the negative repercussions that would almost certainly occur if a woman were killed while flying. He was concerned that aviation would be severely restricted by the government, or by the public itself, if a woman died as a result of taking flight.

Curtiss finally agreed to give her lessons, but his plane did not have room for two people, so he taught from the ground while she sat behind the controls. Despite having a governor on the carburetor, on September 6, 1910, the wind conditions and her ground speed were enough to lift Scott off the ground, much to Curtiss's dismay but Scott's delight. This short flight made her the first woman in the country to have independently flown a plane. Within just a month Scott became part of Curtiss's team, and she flew in a wide variety of exhibitions and competitions until 1916, at which point she had had enough of the dangerous and unpredictable world of exhibition and stunt flying.

An incident in 1912 also greatly affected Blanche. She was flying over Dorchester Bay near Boston as part of a large aerial exhibition and happened to be in a position to see her friend and fellow female pilot Harriet Quimby and Quimby's passenger fall out of their plane and plummet to their deaths. She continued to fly in endurance meets and exhibitions for four more years, during which she had two serious accidents and accumulated a total of 41 broken bones. Upon retirement from active flying she remained significantly involved in the broader business of aeronautics, and accomplished an impressive list of firsts.

In 1911 Scott helped form the Aeronautical Society of Women. The *Chester* (Pennsylvania) *Times* reported in 1912 that she became the nation's first female test pilot. She performed the lead role in the first movie made about flying—*The Aviator's Bride*—and was the first woman to pilot a military jet when, in 1948, she flew with famed pilot Chuck Yeager. Scott continued a life vocation connected with aviation, including working at the U. S. Air Force Museum in Dayton for many years.

Blanche eventually returned to her hometown of Rochester, where she hosted a popular radio show during the 1950s. In one of the more unusual highlights of her life, she received a trophy from television personality Steve Allen on his weekly TV show on January 7, 1955, in recognition of her many accomplishments and years of service, according to a *Chronicle-Express* report. Scott died in 1970 in Rochester after 84 years of living life her way. In 1980 the U.S. Postal Service honored her by issuing the Blanche Stuart Scott air mail stamp, and in 2005 she was inducted into the National Women's Hall of Fame.

SOME OF THE MOST fascinating cutting-edge women involved in motorized adventure in the 1910s were those who took to motorcycles with gusto. Perhaps because they were in such a minority at the time, their exploits seem especially daring and fascinating. Like today, an enthusiastic and dedicated corps of female riders defied the odds and expectations and became full and active participants in the sport.

Women riding solo on their own motorcycles were just uncommon enough to be noteworthy, and newspapers and motorcycle journals frequently wrote about them, often going overboard in the coverage and painting an unfortunately inaccurate picture. Motorcycle journals in particular went out of their way to publish stories about women motorcyclists, stressing the uniqueness of the situation with thinly disguised admiration for those women who rode.

This was especially true in the earliest years of recreational motorcycling when media coverage created the impression that all of the nation's women motorcyclists could be individually identified. *Motor Cycle Illustrated* magazine published an article in 1908 with the headline "Detroit Has Woman Motorcyclist," a heading and story concept that would be unthinkable today.

The article went on to say,

> "The unique distinction of being the only woman motorcyclist between New York and San Francisco is claimed for Mrs. H.G. Smith, of 574 Putnam Ave., Detroit, Mich., wife of the president of the Detroit Motorcycle Club. Mr. Smith has been an ardent motorcyclist for some time, and last summer took Mrs. Smith with him on a run over hills, rocky roads and through peaceful valleys between Detroit and Bayport. When she returned from one of the finest vacation trips imaginable, she was not only a thorough convert to the motorcycle, but decided that instead of merely being a passenger on the rear seat she would handle the levers and brakes herself. Three

months ago she received her new machine, has now thoroughly mastered its mechanism, and accompanied the Detroit M.C. on its recent run."

The Smith motorcycling couple in this article is the same husband and wife duo involved in the 1908 Detroit court case discussed earlier. They did not seek all the attention they received simply because they happened to enjoy riding motorcycles, but because they were active participants in a new phenomenon that caught the public's fancy, they had their proverbial fifteen minutes of fame whether they wanted it or not.

Letter writers to subsequent editions of the magazine made it clear that, no, Mrs. Smith was not the only female motorcyclist between New York and San Francisco. A writer from Minnesota said that his wife also had her own machine, and several other writers in the heartland confirmed that women between the coasts owned and rode their own machines. The mere fact that such statements and correspondence even existed testified to the rarity of women riders in the early years of motorcycles.

Not surprisingly, it seems that some of the early women riders were also active in the suffrage fight. Detroit's Mrs. Smith may have been included in that number based on a white parade uniform she's wearing in one photograph. In reality, far more women were riding motorcycles than early stories such as those about Mrs. Smith suggest. If you read the enthusiast magazines of the time, pictures of appropriately garbed women riders on their motorcycles are commonplace, and women pictured astride various brands of machines were frequently an advertising theme.

WHILE A WOMAN on a motorcycle barely rates a second look today because they're so common, the presence of women in professional motorsports competition is still rare enough that women who do participate in racing are often the subject of much discussion and scrutiny. This aspect of motorcycling hasn't changed much in a hundred years.

The presence of women on America's race tracks in the early 20th century was very uncommon for many reasons beyond gender discrimination. Only a tiny percentage of male riders got involved in racing. It was a dangerous and expensive proposition, and, ultimately, many racers depended on factory sponsorships to compete seriously as professionals. Factories at the time were not inclined to put females on their costly high profile racing teams. Motorcycle competition was a dangerous affair in the early days, and many racers were killed or badly injured.

Manufacturers and race promoters didn't want to chance being connected to the death of a woman racer. After Mrs. J. W. Terhune won a motorcycle hill climbing event near New York City in December 1916, Mr. E. F. Hallock, editor of *Motor Cycle Illustrated*, pondered the presence of women in competitive events. He feared that, when the first woman was killed or seriously injured, the public outcry would negatively impact the sport. He wrote, "Without doubt the girl in competition would add much to the keenness of this contest; but the cost in negative publicity would far outbalance the good results."

Mr. Hallock's concerns were shared by many others, especially manufacturers that did not want the public to sour on the idea of women's recreational use of motorcycles. In those days, society expected men to protect women and keep them from harm. The potential for devastating publicity was just too great and most, but not quite all, manufacturers would not sponsor women racers.

Manufacturers were not ignoring the economic potential of women riders, however. Many advertisements targeted women in a clear attempt to woo their business. Manufacturers realized the value of including women in ads for cars and motorcycles for two reasons. Women bought machines on their own accord and including women broadened the marketplace. Also, once cars and bikes had progressed technologically so that they were attractive to women, companies used this to imply that their equipment had arrived; it was dependable and easy to operate. Such qualities made it desirable to all buyers, regardless of gender.

ONE MOTORCYCLE manufacturer that went the extra mile to target female motorcyclists, and had no qualms about sponsoring a woman racer, was the Wagner Motorcycle Company of St. Paul, Minnesota. Owner George Wagner's daughter Clara was a motorcycling enthusiast and an employee of the corporation, which certainly helps explain the company's open-minded approach toward female riders. In 1909 it was the first and only company to make a motorcycle model specifically designed for women. This idea was so commonsensical that, in retrospect, one wonders why other companies hadn't done it, too. The concept was simple. Make a motorcycle frame that resembled the frame of a woman's bicycle, with a lower brace connecting the front forks and the seat column, rather than having that frame member extend straight across, with the gasoline tank suspended from it as was the norm on motorcycles of the day.

This "Ladies Drop Frame" model had several advantages. The design moved the 2-gallon gas tank from immediately in front of the rider to atop the rear fender behind the seat, completely out of the rider's way. Because women still wore long skirts when riding circa 1910, lowering the frame and moving the gas tank made room for all that clothing. It meant that a woman could get on and off the machine much more easily and certainly more gracefully—an important consideration in those days. Finally, it allowed the saddle to be placed a bit lower, making the machine handle more easily, especially when at a standstill, despite its standard 28-inch wheels. The 3.5 horsepower Ladies' Drop Frame model weighed a svelte 140 pounds and cost $210 dollars in 1909. Practical options available on this model included guards over the chain and spokes, keeping skirts from getting caught in moving parts.

Clara Wagner was another precocious young woman who broke some rules. She was an enthusiastic and skillful rider who was initiated into the sport at an early age and who joined FAM in 1907 at the age of fifteen. By age eighteen, she was working as the bookkeeper in her father's successful and rapidly growing company. With her father's full approval and support, she decided to compete in endurance racing events.

In 1910 Ms. Wagner won such a contest, consisting of over 350 miles of muddy and rough trails, with an unheard-of perfect score. However, when the race officials discovered that she was a woman, they disqualified her, stating that the race had been intended for men only. Clara's male competitors, being more fair-minded and open-minded than the race officials, took up a collection among themselves and bestowed their own award for her obvious and considerable talents.

Her male competitors were fully aware of the great skill and physical and mental toughness that it took to finish the race, let alone win it with a flawless performance.

CLARA WAGNER WAS just one of a few female racers who gained respect and fame in that era and who benefited from corporate sponsorship. Another extraordinary nonconforming and highly skilled young woman was Miss Margaret Gast of New York City. In 1910 she signed a contract with the Flying Merkel Company to race motorcycles on a board track at Miami. Miss Gast and the company formed a long and mutually beneficial relationship after that initial successful venture.

Gast came out of the high speed bicycle racing sport where she had gained fame on wood track venues. She also set astonishing records for long distance endurance bicycling. She was well known in the New York City area, where she lived after emigrating from Germany as a teenager. In 1910 Gast was the only "girl" motordrome racer in the world, performing the same death-defying stunts as male riders and racing with all caution thrown to the wind, as evidenced by her many injuries. Motorcycle racing was a dangerous sport and board track racing was the most dangerous of all. It was also wildly popular.

Racing on machines without brakes on highly banked tracks made of wood boards, at speeds approaching 100 miles per hour and wearing only sweaters and long pants, these daredevils defied death and injury at every turn. Accidents were commonplace, and injuries and even deaths were routine. In addition to frequent racer injuries and fatalities, spectators were also regular victims when out-of-control machines careened off the track at high speeds.

Because of the dangers involved for racer and onlooker alike, the board track rage lasted less than thirty years. As a member of this fearless fraternity, Gast became known as "The Flying Merkel Mile-a-Minute-Girl" and was a fan favorite. In 1914 she toured Canada with the Darnaby Carnival Company, performing her signature wall of death stunts and racing on wood tracks across the continent. She was a special guest at the 1916 FAM convention in New York City, where she entertained convention goers with stunt riding exhibitions.

The Van Buren sisters, who were just about to embark on their historic motorcycle journey across the country, were among those who watched her perform in New York City. She also displayed the 100 medals and trophies she had won in various racing competitions in the U.S. and Canada. *American Motorcyclist* reported that Gast was an incredibly gifted rider and fearless competitor who won the respect of riders, spectators, and fellow competitors.

FRANCES LOEB OF New York City was also a cutting-edge and fearless personality who said "damn the rules." Loeb participated in local events, including endurance races held on Long Island's notoriously difficult sand and mud road courses in the early 1900s. She was an independent racer, not associated with a company team. She was also a loyal Indian enthusiast who took her racing seriously, but who enjoyed recreational motorcycling as well.

On May 5, 1912, Loeb rode in a grueling 200-mile endurance race on Long Island in which she was listed as DNF—did not finish. It's possible that she had a mechanical breakdown, or perhaps she was one of five racers that day who were arrested for speeding in the town of Freeport. The local justice of the peace fined each racer $5, but, by the time they were released, it was too late to complete the race. Such were the realities of road racing in those days.

In October and November 1914 the City of New York celebrated its 300th anniversary with four weeks' worth of parades and special events. As part of this tercentenary observance the city sponsored an automobile pageant with multiple categories, subdivided by automobile and motorcycle divisions, and by gender in each division. Loeb won a first prize in the Motorcycle Division. She was awarded the $25 first-place prize for being "the woman most appropriately dressed for motorcycle riding, and riding and owning her own machine."

Elsewhere in the festivities, Augusta Van Buren was a judge in one of the automobile categories at the pageant, a tribute to the respect she had garnered among the event's organizers. Augusta's judging responsibilities centered on the Advertising Division. She and her cohorts awarded first place to a car decorated by the Omar Cigarette Company. Second place went to an entry by Bull Durham Tobacco, as reported by the *New York Times*.

New York City's gala affair included a spectacular parade comprised of dozens of floats, cars, motorcycles, bands, and all the other attractions typically found in large spectacles such as this, working its way down Madison Avenue to Columbus Circle. Enthusiastic crowds lined the sidewalks and watched from windows high above the motorcade. The parade was held on two different days, to be sure that as many Gothamites as possible could join in the celebration.

The Hendee Manufacturing Company entered a float for its Indian motorcycles called "The Indians of 1614 and 1914," escorted by Indian riders. Groups of motorcyclists rode in the parade, segregated by brand loyalties. It seems quite likely that Loeb and the Van Buren sisters would have participated in such an extraordinary opportunity to ride and to publicly display their Indian allegiance. Effie Hotchkiss may well have ridden one of her older Harley-Davidsons with the Motor Company's contingent. Effie rode with a New York City club whose members owned Harleys, and it's likely that the group would have jumped at the chance to ride in this once in a lifetime experience.

Ms. Loeb gave up motorcycle racing for several years, concentrating on enjoying riding instead of competing. But in the fall of 1916 the racing bug bit her again. *Motor Cycle Illustrated* magazine reported,

> "Ms. Frances Loeb, who a few years ago made quite a name for herself as a competition rider on Indian machines, has decided to come back. Baker, Murray & Imbrie, New York Indian distributors, have sold Ms. Loeb a new Indian outfit which she expects to ride in endurance runs and other contests during the coming season."

As large as New York City was back then, the sorority of female motorcyclists there was quite small in numbers. The number of women who were very serious riders or who raced competitively was smaller still. As a result, it is fairly likely that members of this unique bloc would have known many of their sister riders, especially if they rode the same brand of machine. Thus I can easily imagine the Van Buren sisters and Ms. Loeb riding together on occasion.

The Baker, Murray & Imbrie Indian agency was a popular destination and hangout for New York City Indian riders. The Van Burens and Loeb were frequent visitors, and it's quite likely that they compared notes and exchanged tips in the agency's lounge, or shared tales of their adventures in front of the warm fire that the dealer kept burning for winter riders.

MISS ETHEL "CY" WOODMAN, a young freelance newspaper reporter from the Long Island village of Sayville, attempted a cross-country excursion in 1913 on a 4-horsepower Flanders motorcycle. Legend has it that Woodman attempted the trip based on a dare and a bet. She is certainly another example of Victorian nonconformity. Woodman nearly reached her goal, but an emergency appendectomy in New Mexico kept her out of the record books, forcing her to abandon the effort and finish the trip to California on a train.

And there was actress Ruth McCord, who made headlines in 1917 by setting off on a motorcycle from Los Angeles on what she had intended to be a 25,000-mile trip around the circumference of America. The record doesn't reflect how much of her goal she accomplished, but having the confidence to even plan and attempt an unprecedented goal as ambitious as hers is testimony to her abilities and courage. The Hendee Manufacturing Company had enough confidence in McCord to prominently depict her aboard an Indian in its advertisements, boasting of her choice of its equipment for her epic journey.

Sometimes breaking the rules isn't a bad thing.

Della Crewe – A Small Town Girl
with Big Dreams

─◦◦◦─

It's a long way to Tipperary,
It's a long way to go.
It's a long way to Tipperary
To the sweetest girl I know!
Goodbye Piccadilly,
Farewell Leicester Square!
It's a long long way to Tipperary,
But my heart's right there.[1]

Miss Della Crewe was a girl from Wisconsin who wanted to see the world, and she pursued that dream with the tenacity and daring that are the hallmark of true explorers. We know almost nothing about her childhood except that her father was a carpenter. What the published record does show is that she left her hometown of Racine behind and, by 1912 at the age of 28, had already journeyed across most of America. She had also spent seven months in Panama, watching history happening during construction of the canal connecting the Atlantic and Pacific oceans.

Miss Crewe's reason for being there isn't known for certain. Maybe she was simply curious and decided to spend a few months in a place that had been in the headlines so often over the previous decade, or perhaps opportunity had knocked and she had cheerfully opened the

---

[1] Lyrics by Jack Judge, 1912

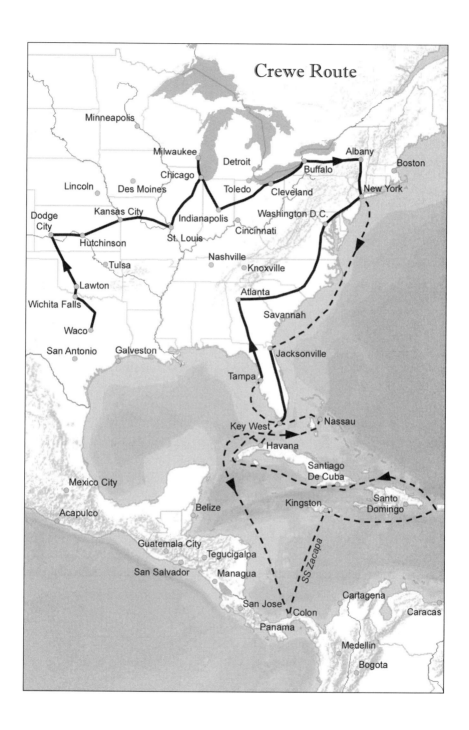

door. After all, she was not the kind of person who would turn down a chance to travel to an exotic location.

In any event, her sojourn in Panama came to an end in the early summer of 1912, and it was time to head back to the states for even more travel opportunities. Departing from the steamy port of Colon in the Canal Zone, she returned to the states via the SS *Abangarez*, one of many United Fruit Company steamer ships used to transport both passengers and freight.

She arrived at the port of New Orleans on July 2 and wandered the streets of a city that was as different in feel, culture, and appearance from her hometown of Racine as any city in a faraway foreign country. From New Orleans, Della went to Muskogee, Oklahoma, and yet another vastly different culture. She was the guest of a family friend and spent two weeks relaxing and learning more about the state that had just been admitted into the union five years earlier.

From Oklahoma Crewe proceeded north to Chicago and, after a bit of sightseeing in the Windy City, stopped in her home town of Racine before departing for Alaska. The young world trekker was well versed in ship and rail transportation and used both in her exploration of North America in that year.

It appears that it was during the brief visit to her home town that her nephew convinced her to give motorcycling a try. Knowing how she loved to travel and explore, he suggested that it would be a great way to see the world. He had planted the seed in a very fertile mind.

By the summer of 1913, Miss Crewe was living in Waco, Texas, where she was employed by a magazine publisher. The tiny seed of using a motorcycle for transportation had sprouted into a large and healthy plant. She purchased one of her own and fell in love with the joys of experiencing the world around her without the hindrance of glass and steel walls. According to the *Elyria* (Ohio) *Evening Telegram*, it was in late 1913 that she announced her intention to journey around the world on one of these marvelous machines, departing from Waco in the summer of 1914.

With the innocence of a pre–World War I American mindset and without the constraints of marriage and family, Della planned to devote three years to her epic adventure, traveling throughout the Orient, Europe, and North America. The *Hutchinson* (Kansas) *News* reported that her initial, thoroughly-thought-out itinerary called for a round-about trip that took her first from Waco to New York with many stops in between. From there she would cross the continent on the Lincoln Highway to San Francisco, where she would board a steamer for Japan. She would ride her cycle across Asia and Europe; then sail to Panama and through the just-opened Panama Canal, taking the ship along the Pacific coast to California. She would head north along America's west coast to British Columbia, ride east through Canada, and ultimately back south to Texas and home.

All in all, it was an ambitious agenda, but the timing seemed perfect. Motorcycles had evolved to the point that bikers could rely on them for long-distance travel in relative comfort and could find dealers and repair shops in many cities. Rapidly improving tire and inner tube technology had largely eliminated frequent flat tires. Perhaps most importantly, conditions around the world when she made her announcement in late 1913 seemed to make it an opportune time for such a trip.

For the first time in many years the world's major nations, especially in Europe, were largely at peace or at least not in a shooting war. Following the Spanish-American War, America's presence and influence had spread to many nations, and American tourists were driving the roads of Europe and sightseeing in far-flung areas of the globe. As long as one avoided some unstable countries, including several in Central America, one could go great distances and not encounter hostilities.

To say the least, Della had become an enthusiastic motorcyclist. During the course of her trip, she was often asked why she was making such an epic journey at all and why she was attempting this seemingly impossible adventure on a motorcycle.

She explained it this way to the *Elyria Evening Telegram*:

> "Well, I love nature better than beautiful clothes or luxuries, and I decided that I would enjoy a trip of this kind more than anything else. It is the call of the road I suppose. Although I have traveled a great deal, I have never derived so much enjoyment from traveling as I have since I started on this tour last June."

Miss Crewe later told a reporter for the _Hartford_ (Connecticut) _Courant_ that it was primarily a sightseeing excursion. She said she chose the motorcycle because she needed to live outdoors and believed that the two-wheeler offered the most convenient and most economical means of transportation.

NEWSPAPER ACCOUNTS at the time of Crewe's and other women's trips provide an interesting insight into the prevailing attitudes toward young women a century ago. Although Della was 29 years old when she made her announcement, headlines in several newspapers that carried the story were very similar to what the _Elyria Evening Telegram_ used, declaring in large type "Girl Motorcyclist To Tour World."

The term "girl" was commonly used when describing young women of the era, and was even used by women who certainly thought of themselves as adults. In her January 1915 interview with the _Hartford Courant_, Crewe herself used the term when talking about her experiences. She said, "I recommend the motorcycle to any girl as a means of recreation. I have gained steadily in health since starting on this trip, and find no difficulty whatever in operating the machine."

The use of "girl" was indicative of the notion that females were not the complete equal of males and it ran deep in societal roots circa 1915. The frequent use of the "gentle sex," the "fair sex," and the "weaker sex," and other similar words or phrases reflected society's view that women in fact differed from males in their physical abilities.

Newspaper and magazine articles at the time seemed filled with amazement that these women were able to pull off activities that were, quite obviously to them, the domain of the male gender. The term "masculinist" was frequently used at the time in reference to men who staunchly held the opinion that there should be a clear delineation of duties and activities according to gender. However, traditions and attitudes were changing quite dramatically during that unique period between the Victorian Era and the Roaring Twenties; too fast for some, not fast enough for others.

IN PREPARATION FOR THE TRIP, Crewe took on an apprenticeship at a Waco motorcycle dealer where she learned the mechanical aspects of the machines and how to repair them. When she wasn't working

A Harley-Davidson motorcycle and sidecar combination, the same model ridden by Crewe during her 1914 / 1915 travels. The sidecar provided adequate room for spare clothing, supplies, tools, and her dog Trouble. (photo by author)

at the shop, or at her primary job as a writer and illustrator, she was riding the roads in the countryside around Waco on her Harley-Davidson motorcycle.

Crewe outfitted her bike with a matching Harley-Davidson sidecar to enable her to carry the gear and supplies needed for an extended trip. The car would also carry two passengers, one being an Irish Bulldog pup named "Trouble," given to her by Waco Board of Trade members so that she would have a companion and, once the pup matured, protection. "Great name, isn't it?" she joked with a *Hutchinson News* reporter. "I hope he'll be the only trouble I have."

Trouble wasn't Crewe's only passenger, though. Newspapers that covered the beginning of her trip noted that she was also carrying a young man described as "a semi-invalid." The *Wichita Falls Daily Times* in Texas also reported on July 3 that Crewe was carrying this young man "to an eastern point."

The paper went on to record that, with all her gear and the passenger, her rig weighed between 600 and 700 pounds. To operate such a motorcycle-sidecar rig with that amount of weight and bulk on the mud trails of the time was truly a Herculean feat given the state of technology in the 1910s!

Of course, the machine had a "kick start" mechanism to fire the engine. Electric start motorcycles were still a distant dream. The kick start apparatus was a clever design. Many motorcycles of that era, including Crewe's 1914 Harley-Davidson, had what looked very much like bicycle pedals. To start the machine, the operator sat on the seat and pedaled vigorously, but instead of turning the rear wheel the pedals were cranking the finicky engine.

Once started, these early machines required the rider to manually adjust what today is handled by computers—spark timing, choke settings, fuel/air ratios, and more. One did not simply get on, push the starter button and ride away as motorcyclists do today.

Virtually all of the motorcycles of that period, including the popular Indian and Harley-Davidson brands, utilized a gear shifting mechanism that eventually earned the nickname "suicide clutch" or "suicide shifter." On a modern motorcycle, the clutch lever is located on the handlebar and is operated by the left hand. The hand does not leave the handlebar, and the rider can maintain stability while shifting gears with the left foot, in a simple up or down movement of the heel or toe of the rider's boot. Once the technique is mastered, the rider can do it virtually without conscious thought and maintain full control of the bike at all times.

That was not the case with motorcycles 100 years ago. Riders shifted transmission gears with a lever located on the side of the gas tank. To operate it, one had to take his or her hand off the handlebar and move the shifter lever, while simultaneously working the clutch with the left foot. If the rider suddenly hit a rock or patch of mud while shifting gears, loss of control was a very likely result.

It also meant that the foot normally used to stabilize the motorcycle, either at a standstill or moving through rough terrain at slow speed, was operating the clutch. Given the fairly narrow power band of the early single or twin-cylinder engines, shifting gears and working the clutch were frequent tasks. Operating machines with that type of mechanism on rough or muddy roads and with a fully-loaded sidecar attached was not for the faint of heart!

WHEN DELLA'S PLANNED departure date arrived, she found it impossible to leave. Recent storms had inundated north Texas, making most roads impassable and washing out many bridges. So she waited until Mother Nature was a bit more cooperative. On the morning of June 23, 1914, she left Waco in the sticky humidity and heat of a Texas summer, eager and excited, but also conscious of the trouble she would probably encounter on such a trip. She traveled on what was called The Meridian Road north from Waco, through Wichita Falls, and across vast wide open spaces to Enid, Oklahoma. From there she rode the lightly traveled and poorly maintained Albert Pike Highway to Dodge City. As was the case for all of America circa 1915, the word "highway" attached to a road carried no guarantees of solid surfaces or regular maintenance.

Crewe described the conditions upon her departure as a "beautiful day overhead, but black gumbo beneath." Most people would have considered the roads to be still impassable, but Miss Crewe wasn't most people.

In regions with gumbo soil, the top several inches of soil can become a viscous mud, making travel by foot or machinery very difficult, while the soil below the gumbo can be dry and hard because water can't make its way beyond the surface clay barrier.

Gumbo soil is especially common in the North American Corn Belt and eastern Plains. Many early twentieth century travelers, whether riding on two wheels or four, were greatly impacted by gumbo mud when hard dusty clay surfaces suddenly became impassible after a rain event.

CREWE'S EXHILARATION was tempered with at least some

Gumbo

GUMBO, in this case, is not a delicious soup, but a technical term used by scientists to classify soil. It's generally a fertile soil for crops, but turns into a thick, sticky mud when wet because of its high clay content. The clay also serves as an impermeable barrier, causing rainwater to pond on the surface rather than soak down into the soil. This "ponding" intensifies the process of mud formation.

realistic anticipation of what the next three years would hold, but she seemed remarkably confident in her ability to achieve her goal. In her pocket she carried a letter of introduction from Secretary of State William Jennings Bryan, in which he encouraged diplomatic personnel to help her as necessary.

In the exquisite diplomatic language of the day, Secretary Bryan wrote, "*I take pleasure in introducing to you Miss Della Crewe of Waco, Texas, who is proceeding abroad, and I cordially bespeak for her such courtesies and assistance as you may be able to render consistent with your official duties.*" A magazine publisher for whom she did some writing pulled strings to get the diplomatic letter. She makes no reference to ever needing to use the letter, but just having it must have been of considerable comfort as she journeyed.

CREWE'S TRIP PLANS were leisurely and filled with frequent stops. She planned to do much exploring and gather lots of information along the way. In fact, she expected to cover much of her costs by writing articles for various magazines.

I've found no official record of a relationship between Della Crewe and the Texaco Corporation, which might have included financial help or perhaps gasoline and oil, but it appears that such an agreement did exist. Photographs of Della on her motorcycle clearly depict the Texaco star logo prominently displayed on the front fork just below the headlight.

She also wrote an article for *The Texaco Star* newsletter, in which she made frequent, praiseworthy reference to her use of Texaco products throughout her trip. She also mentioned stopping at many Texaco facilities in the U.S. and abroad to meet with company representatives.

Such an arrangement would not have been the least bit unusual. Many companies were anxious to have their name connected with the various cutting edge adventures of that era. Having one's brand connected with a difficult effort that succeeded was an effective way of promoting the capabilities of their products. Many early adventure travelers made full use of corporate sponsorship.

Alice Ramsey, who drove a Maxwell car free of cost as a promotional venture by the factory, was one of the first. Actress Anita King's

Kissel Kar looked like a rolling billboard as she drove the donated vehicle from San Francisco to New York in 1915. A banner on the side read Koast to Koast in a Kissel Kar. A year later, a combination of backers, including the YWCA, The Oldsmobile Motor Company, and the Lincoln Highway Association sponsored Miss Amanda Preuss's trip across America from California to New York by providing her with a well-marked Oldsmobile.

It was a costly affair to purchase and properly equip a vehicle for transcontinental travel, and the costs of repairs would have been significant. In some instances, sponsorship also helped ensure that services would be available along the way in the form of gasoline and oil, tires, repair facilities, and publicity for the sponsor and driver.

CREWE'S FIRST SEVERAL days on the road presented a stark preview of what awaited her in the world of 1914, when even poorly maintained roads were a future development. She struggled mightily to get her motorcycle and sidecar through the muddy trails of Texas and Oklahoma. Early summer rains had left the roads a quagmire. She hit a tree stump in Oklahoma after slipping on a muddy road, damaging her sidecar. As she told a *Hutchinson News* reporter, "I have had the worst time getting through from Waco to Dodge City. Those Texas roads are awful."

She went on to say that the roads in Kansas were dry and "heavenly" by comparison. Motoring across Kansas under an immense blue sky, the likes of which can only be truly appreciated in the North American prairies, Della felt that her dream was really coming true. A smile spread across her face as she rode through the vast silence.

Slowly but steadily she motored down the narrow trails that cut through fields of wheat transitioning from amber to brown. She passed occasional farm houses with chickens in the yards and kids who chased after her as far as they could before they finally ran out of breath or got beyond of the watchful eyes of their mothers.

It was a powerful feeling of freedom and adventure, and that's what the trip was all about. We can only imagine the many fascinating interactions and conversations that occurred when Crewe and other women met strangers along the road or in the small towns that dotted the vast open spaces of America. It must have been a struggle to break

free from the many people who wanted to talk to these interesting women and hear all about their unique mode of transportation and their marvelous adventures.

To this day, one unique and positive feature of motorcycle travel is that many strangers will go out of their way to talk with riders, especially those who are obviously on a long distance trip. Even many people who wouldn't get on a motorcycle on a dare are fascinated by this unique way to see the world and enjoy hearing about the travels and adventures of motorcyclists.

THE FIRST MAJOR STOP on Crewe's agenda was Dodge City, Kansas, to watch the motorcycle races on Independence Day, which had already become established as one of the premier events of the season. Della had special reason to attend because the first-ever 300-mile "Coyote Classic" was to be held at the high-banked, two-mile dirt track. Once again she wanted to be a witness to history.

It was also the first major event at which the Harley-Davidson Motor Company—Crewe's adopted brand—was to make a concerted effort. Although private owners used Harley-Davidson machines in various types of racing venues, the company had stated in advertisements prior to 1915 that they made machines for riding, not racing. Harley-Davidson was happy with the results of the Dodge City event and the attention it brought, and thus began the Milwaukee-based company's long and illustrious racing program. Just one year later, Harley-Davidson won the 1915 Dodge City race, and took six of the top seven places.

Besides the H-D squad, teams representing Excelsior, Merkel, Pope, Thor and Indian brands also competed. Crewe may have been disappointed that Glen Boyd, riding an Indian, got the checkered flag, but she and thousands of other enthusiastic spectators enjoyed a spectacular run, and the Dodge City venue became a fixture in the American motorcycle racing scene for decades.

UPON LEAVING Dodge City, Crewe rode to nearby Sterling, Kansas, "where she stopped a couple of days to visit her sister, Mrs. T. A. Rogers," according to a *Hutchinson News* item. It appears that Crewe and her young invalid passenger parted company at Sterling, if not before, because no reference whatsoever is made to this unidentified young man from this point onward. She lost his companionship, but his departure must have made her journey much easier!

From Sterling, she rode through Hutchinson and Kansas City, then on to St. Louis for the Federation of American Motorcyclists Convention. Crewe planned to spend at least four days in St. Louis attending the annual meeting July 15–18. She was a member of the FAM, as well as the Waco Motorcycle Club.

Since its founding in 1903, the federation had become a powerful voice for the rights of motorcyclists and motorcycling in American society. FAM was also the sanctioning authority for a wide variety of events and races.

Della arrived at St. Louis' Planter's Hotel, home of the convention, on July 15 along with 1,500 other motorcyclists. That the convention was held at the Planter's is noteworthy because it was regarded as the finest hotel in the city. Nothing was considered too extravagant for this building, which was a symbol of the sophistication and status of this important Midwestern city. By then, the FAM was an organization with significant financial backing and influence and was able

Harley-Davidson
Again Wins at Dodge City

The World's Motorcycle Classic of 300 miles at Dodge City was won by Jim Davis on his pocket valve Harley-Davidson, in 3 hours, 40 minutes and 4⁴⁵ seconds.

New World's Record

The pulse of the motorcycle world has been at high tension ever since the announcement that the greatest of all races would be resumed on the Dodge City two-mile track. Winning this meant the crowning speedway achievement of the year 1920. The keen rivalry in the competing camps urged the battling riders to a record-breaking speed — Davis cutting 5 minutes, 31 1-5 seconds off the former world's record for a dirt track.

300-Mile Title Held by Harley-Davidson Since 1915

1915-Otto Walker,	*Harley Davidson,*	Time	3:55:45
1916-Irving Janke,	*Harley Davidson,*	Time	3:45:36
1917-1918-1919	. . . . . .	No Races Held	
1920-Jim Davis	*Harley Davidson*	Time	3:40:04 4-5

JIM DAVIS
Winner of the Dodge City Classic, July 5th, 1920

The Harley-Davidson Has Won Every Long Distance Race Held During the Past 2 Years

HARLEY-DAVIDSON MOTOR CO.
MILWAUKEE, U. S. A.
Largest Producer of Motorcycles in the World

to book the iconic hotel. It had grown into a powerful force, with 27,687 members at the time, according to records published by *The Washington Post*.

The St. Louis *Globe-Democrat* noted that most of the FAM attendees arrived by train. The road system was so decrepit and undependable in 1914 that even most die-hard motorcyclists traveled by train rather than attempt to motorcycle to their own event! However, one family did not ride the rails. The federation's president—Dr. B. J. Patterson, of Kansas City—rode his motorcycle to St. Louis. His wife rode in a side car attached to her daughter's cycle.

The gathering was a prestigious and money-making event for St. Louis, and planners scheduled a parade and races to enhance the affair. In a unique twist, Dr. Patterson arranged to have the marching band ride in sidecars as part of the parade. This first-ever approach to such a performance went off without a hitch, and press accounts indicate that spectators enjoyed it very much.

IN ADDITION TO the meetings that occur at any convention, two additional events headlined the schedule. One was an endurance run by a group of motorcyclists riding from Chicago to St. Louis. Those riders found it very difficult, but most were able to finish. However, all riders with sidecars attached to their machines failed to make it because they could not find their way around a washed out bridge that they encountered.

Many riders who went to the convention on their machines noted the deplorable road conditions, and two Logansport, Indiana, men left impressions of what they had to endure. An article in the *St. Louis Post Dispatch* reported, "They claim no one ever drove a machine over worse roads in as much as Illinois has no gravel or stone roads and all are either dirt or sand, in many places the dust was 8 to 10 inches deep." One begins to understand why so many enthusiasts took the train rather than risk breaking down or getting stuck in the barely passable trails that led to St. Louis.

The second event staged for attendees involved watching motorcycle races at the Maxwelton Track located on the St. Charles Rock Road west of town. The one mile dirt track was reputed to be a very fast

Flesh and blood horsepower often came to the rescue when drivers found themselves hopelessly mired in the deep mud of circa 1915 America. Crewe experienced these conditions much of the way during the summer of 1914 as she traveled from Waco, Texas to Racine, Wisconsin. (Photo used by permission. University of Michigan / Bentley Library)

venue and made viewing exciting for spectators, though dangerous riding for competitors. At least one rider was killed during the 1914 race.

Miss Crewe went from St. Louis to Chicago, likely having to follow many of the same difficult trails that the endurance team complained about. However, she was not participating in an endurance run, so she could relax a bit and enjoy the trip.

It was a good thing that Della was able to slow down and take her time. The Midwest was experiencing one of its renowned July heat waves, and temperatures in that part of the country exceeded 100°. Trouble the bulldog enjoyed sitting up tall with the wind in his face, though a few months later he would burrow deep in the sidecar to find warmth out of the wind.

For three hundred miles Crewe rode past fields of waist-high corn and dark green, blossoming soybeans, and along fenced pastures where wide-eyed curious cows stared at the strange sight. From Chicago she continued north to Racine and Milwaukee. While the Harley-Davidson factory was making some repairs and adjustments to her motorcycle and sidecar in preparation for her extended journey, she stayed at her mother's home on Hayes Street in nearby Racine.

THROUGH AN EXTENSIVE interview with a *Racine Journal-News* reporter, we are able to learn more about Della Crewe's travels. Prior to this trip she had "spent considerable time in Alaska, and has traveled extensively in practically every part of the union." She was described as being a magazine writer and illustrator. She also was reportedly gathering information along the way to write a book called "Rural Life in America," but I have found no record for a book by this title and author.

Della spent several weeks in Racine, where she had to make some difficult decisions about alterations to her extensive travel plans because of unexpected "European trouble". You see, just five days after she left Waco, an event in Sarajevo, Serbia, had had an immeasurable impact on the world at large and certainly on her trip.

When an anarchist's bullets killed Archduke Franz Ferdinand—heir apparent to the Austro-Hungarian throne—and his wife the Duchess Sophie, the world changed. The assassinations affected the lives of millions for decades to come, and killed millions more in the interim.

By the time Della reached Wisconsin, it was obvious that travel to Europe was going to be impossible for the foreseeable future. Comments reported by newspapers made it clear that Crewe was weighing her options and considering alternatives that would keep her out of Europe.

IN AN INTERESTING and quite extraordinary coincidence, another motorcyclist, living in Wisconsin while attending university in Madison, was likewise dramatically affected by events in Europe. But Rachel Foster Avery's story began long before the tumultuous summer of 1914.

Rachel was born in Pittsburgh in 1858, the daughter of parents who brought the outside world into their home for her to observe from an early age. Her father was a newspaper editor, and her mother was actively involved in early women's suffrage efforts. This out-of-the-ordinary upbringing probably played a major role in forming Rachel's expansive view of social and political issues.

At 23 years old Rachel became associated with Susan B. Anthony and the national suffrage movement. In 1888 she formed the International Council of Women and married Cyrus Avery. She toured Europe with Anthony to meet with European leaders in the women's rights movement, and quickly became the famous suffragette's most trusted assistant. Rachel served in suffrage organization leadership roles for two decades, and was instrumental in setting policies and moving the initiative forward.

In 1910 Mrs. Avery decided it was time to leave center stage and move on to other interests that she had been keeping on the back burner, including buying a motorcycle. She attended the Pennsylvania College of Agriculture for two years and then moved, along with her daughters Julia and Rose, to Wisconsin where they enrolled in its state university's four year agricultural program.

Julia was to become Rachel's motorcycling partner. Of her enrollment in agricultural studies, the *Oshkosh Daily Northwestern* reported that Julia was "secretary of the junior class, a gifted fancy dancer, an all around athlete, and an able student in a course most women find difficult." But Rachel and Julia weren't going to let a newspaper reporter's outdated beliefs about a woman's capabilities influence their plans.

AT THE END OF the 1914 spring semester they immediately departed for Europe with their motorcycle and sidecar to tour the continent. They intended to research agricultural practices in several western European countries. Of course the trip would not be all work; Rachel described it as "a two month open air picnic."

Unfortunately, their timing could not have been worse. In August they were stopped by military officials in Belgium, and their motorcycle was confiscated for war use. Germany invaded Belgium on August 3, and the Belgians were in a desperate fight to stop Germany's advance into their homeland. A motorcycle and sidecar would have been a valuable asset for the ill-equipped Belgian military.

In the summer of 1914 thousands of Americans found themselves stranded in Europe by the sudden outbreak of an unexpected war. In

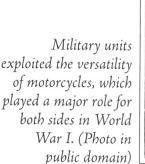

Military units exploited the versatility of motorcycles, which played a major role for both sides in World War I. (Photo in public domain)

late August newspapers reported that 11,000 American refugees were being brought back on International Mercantile Marine Lines steamers. The first of many ships chartered for this purpose arrived in New York on August 24. Mother and daughter eventually made it back to the states, sans their motorcycle and sidecar. Having seen history in the making on such a personal level, stories about their amazing European adventures provided entertainment fodder at dinner parties and family gatherings for years to come!

Deciding that it was finally time to settle down and pursue a dream of land ownership, Rachel bought a farm in Bucks County, Pennsylvania, in 1915. She was warmly received in the rural community. According to the *New Castle News*, male farmers in the area applauded her and her history of fighting for women's suffrage, with one farmer going on record to say, "If women have brains enough to manage a farm, they certainly have brains enough to vote."

Unfortunately, she did not live long after moving to her modern farm. She died in October 1919, just four months after Congress passed the proposed 19th Amendment to the Constitution which, if approved by the states, would guarantee women's right to vote in all elections. This law was the culmination of her life's work, but she died wondering if the necessary 36 states would approve the measure to make it the law of the land.

Such approval by state legislatures was by no means certain. However, on August 18, 1920, Tennessee became the final state to approve the proposal...by a single vote. Twenty-four year old legislator Harry Burns, under pressure from his mother to support amendment, was the "good boy" she had urged him to be and cast the deciding yes vote. The amendment took effect August 26, 1920, and women were able to vote in that fall's general election. Another chapter in America's long and fascinating history had been written.

THE ODDS ARE GREAT that Della Crewe heard about the Averies' predicament in Europe. Back home in Racine, she was well aware of the turmoil that was suddenly transforming Europe from a traveler's delight to a place of danger and uncertainty.

With Austria-Hungary's formal declaration of war against Serbia on July 28 and Germany's invasions of France and Belgium the following week, things took a sudden and dangerous turn for the worse. Reports of American tourists and business travelers in Europe being turned overnight into refugees would be enough to cause her to decide to revise her plans and stay closer to home. The September 6 *New York Times* carried an article describing both the Avery situation and Della's changed travel itinerary. Crewe reported that she would continue her trip to New York, and then travel to safe parts of Central and South America.

Not all was well in the Western Hemisphere either circa 1914. Dangerous revolts were brewing in Nicaragua, Honduras, Mexico, Haiti, and the Dominican Republic, and journeying through those countries could have been life-threatening. The U.S. Marines were sent into Haiti and the Dominican Republic to suppress revolts and help restore order. Revolution brewing in Mexico would blossom into a near war with the United States in the coming years, and deadly insurgencies in Central America made conditions dangerous for everyone, native or foreign.

Miss Crewe hoped that, once she completed her journeys throughout the U.S. and several safe Caribbean nations, conditions in Europe would have returned to normal. In that case, she planned to go back to New York, ride cross-country to San Francisco, then sail to the Orient, all according to her original itinerary, as reported in the *New York Times*.

DESPITE THE gathering cold of early November, Della left Wisconsin and rode south to Indianapolis, arriving there on November 5. Her dog Trouble proved to be of some trouble after all because he was suffering from a bad case of mange, and this caught the attention of Indiana agricultural officials. The state was under quarantine for hoof and mouth disease, and she was stopped twice because of her dog's condition. Assurances that she was just passing through and that she would not let Trouble out of the sidecar satisfied officials, and she was allowed to continue on her way. To keep Trouble warm during the time he had lost much of his hair to mange, she fitted him with a specially made sweater.

It's unclear why Crewe went out of her way to Indianapolis that late in the season, but she enjoyed making numerous side trips and did not stick with a point-to-point travel scheme. From Indy she went through Marion, Ohio, and into northeastern Ohio, where the weather had already turned cold and snowy. A grainy newspaper photograph shows her riding in the snow during the winter of 1914-1915. Few motorcyclists of either gender ride in those conditions today.

Various latter day written accounts tell a story about Crewe that occurred in northeastern Ohio's "snow belt," where cold winds blowing off Lake Erie often create blizzard-like conditions. Caught in a snowstorm, she reportedly came upon a farmhouse, but the farmer supposedly refused to allow her to come in because he felt that she shouldn't be out in such conditions by herself in the first place. The story has it that, only when the farmer's wife interceded on behalf of the frozen travelers were Della and Trouble provided warm shelter.

It is easy to imagine a stern farmer, used to a hard life and following a strict code of work and proper behavior, chastising the strong-willed Miss Crewe for being unorthodox. However, it is difficult to believe that this same upright citizen could, for a moment, deny anyone safety and warmth in such dire circumstances. One of the basic unwritten codes of conduct, obvious from reading many accounts of trips during that time, was that people offered ready, open arms and doors to travelers, especially women, in need of shelter or help.

FROM VARIOUS REPORTS of the period, chivalry was in fact alive, and respect for women was a well-established principle in society. Of course, admiration alone was not the same as equal rights in the legal sense, but it did mean that even men who had no respect for another man or another man's property would think twice about being disrespectful to a woman. This ingrained attitude is why it was possible for young women such as Crewe to travel virtually anywhere they chose without undue fear. All of the women of this book exhibited the same confident attitude about their safety on the road and of the deference they assumed they would be shown.

This societal attitude was one of the positive results of the Victorian Age. It allowed women to travel safely in places that we today assume would have been too dangerous. A little-known book written by a female traveler in the Rocky Mountains during the height of 19th century Wild West days provides excellent documentation.

A Lady's Life in the Rocky Mountains is a compilation of letters that Miss Isabella Bird wrote to family and friends in England. The letters span several years and describe in wonderful detail her solitary journey in the Rockies during the 1870s and 1880s. She writes about traveling alone, or with a local male guide familiar with the area, without any hesitation whatsoever.

In one of her earliest letters, Miss Bird tells of going by train in 1873 to the lawless town of Truckee, California. She portrays a ramshackle village filled with crude and lawless men who sought out frontier life as a means of escaping the restraints of civilization. Yet in this town, filled with men who would shoot another man without a second thought if they believed they had been cheated in a card game, she had no concerns about walking around unescorted or even of renting a horse to take a solitary ride deep into the surrounding forests.

The only scare Miss Bird had was when a grizzly bear reared up in front of her on the trail, spooking her horse and leaving her lying bruised on the ground several miles from civilization. In time a woodcutter came by, holding her horse by the reins, and helped her back to town. She goes on to tell of many similar occurrences in Colorado and Wyoming when she correctly assumed that the men around her held her in great esteem and would never harm her.

Two years after Miss Crewe began her monumental solitary motorcycle journey, Augusta Van Buren, on her own cross-country motorcycle trip, remarked:

"People who are at a loss to know how two young women can get along without a man to protect them from the hard knocks of the world have a mistaken idea of what kind of a place the world really is. Everybody has been perfectly lovely. We have placed confidence in people, and they have lived up to their trust."

This remark, reported by the Springfield, Massachusetts, *Daily Republican*, seemed to summarize perfectly the attitude that daring women of the time had, and that must have added greatly to their confidence. Adeline Van Buren echoed this same confidence in their safety and acceptance by the people in Salt Lake City. After more than six weeks on the road, she and her sister Augusta had had no problems with the people they had met along the way. When a reporter from the *Salt Lake Telegram* asked the sisters whether they had encountered any "annoyances," Adeline responded, "Annoyances? Certainly not! We are traveling in America."

AFTER WHAT WOULD have been a superhuman effort to cross the Great Lakes region and New York State during the early winter, Miss Crewe arrived in New York City on December 12, 1914. She described conditions as being ten degrees above zero and that she was "weighted down with four pairs of stockings, sheep skin, storm shoes, heavy dress, one sweater, two coats, two hoods." Crewe went on to say that a New York City Harley-Davidson dealer "built up a roaring fire which melted away the remains of snow and ice storms encountered on the road." She also had high praise for her machine, telling a *Hutchinson News* reporter, "Thaws, slush, fresh gravel, ice and snow made little difference to my motor."

While in New York City, Della was able to finalize her alternate plans and make the necessary arrangements. In an interesting coincidence, on December 13, 1914 the Sunday *New York Times* ran a series of articles extolling the pleasures of several Caribbean islands and the Panama Canal Zone. The *Times* was recommending Porto Rico (as it was spelled then), Cuba, and Panama as "safe and warm destinations for winter travelers whose European plans had to be cancelled." Though it seems that she had already devised an itinerary for island hopping in the Caribbean, this newspaper coverage may have provided her with the satisfaction that she had chosen well.

It seems that she may have parted company with Trouble prior to leaving New York as no one mentions the dog during her travels in the Caribbean region. She would have had to deal with several foreign governments to get necessary paperwork for an animal, which would have been prohibitively complicated and time-consuming.

Crewe spent close to a month in New York City before sailing with her bike on a steamship down the Atlantic coast to Florida. How other passengers and crew members must have gathered around her for a chance to talk to this fascinating young woman and hear all about her travels and motorcycling adventures! She would have garnered a great deal of attention, and her conversations with other seasoned travelers gave her insight into the practicalities of travel in the Caribbean and about its many attractions.

From Key West she sailed to Havana, Cuba. No account remains of the time she spent in Cuba or how much of it she was able to visit, but one can just imagine that she took in all the sights she could, given her expansive attitude about travel and exploration. One newspaper article simply reported that she "toured Cuba," which suggests that she made much more than a quick stop in Havana.

From Cuba Della sailed to Panama, where she was met by the president of the Canal Zone Motorcycle Club. Upon arriving at Colon, she noted that she had two hundred miles of roads to ride. One attraction that Crewe and members of the club saw was the Big Chief Monument at the Mount Hope U.S. Government Burial Grounds.

Having previously lived in Panama, she knew the country well. She spent a week getting around, visiting many friends and acquaintances. From Colon, she sailed to Jamaica on the SS *Zacapa*—another United Fruit Company steamship. Captain Law guided the *Zacapa* on the two day sail and reported that they "had a splendid trip down."

Jamaica—the "Gem of the Caribbean"—was clearly a favorite of Crewe's various stops on the trip, and the island's newspaper covered her time there in great detail. She stayed in Kingston for six days, riding local roads on her motorcycle, seeing the sights, and attracting much attention from the locals.

Della wrote that she intended to stay at the Myrtle Bank Hotel while in Kingston, but that was premature. The hotel, one of the nicest on the island, was destroyed in a 1907 earthquake and not rebuilt until 1918. Otherwise, Crewe was most positive in her description of the island and its people, telling a *Gleaner* reporter, "Everywhere I have been to everybody has met me with the greatest courtesy and the people simply lovely. I am taking in the neutral countries in my tour. I think it is an ideal way of seeing the world by motorcycle."

She also told the reporter that she had thus far ridden 276 miles of "the beautiful roads of Jamaica" and that she was enjoying the scenery very much. Indeed, the luxuriant greenery of the island and the sights and smells she encountered while riding through rolling forests of bamboo and palms were a feast for the senses. She was fully immersed in the warm scent-filled air that surrounded her as she motored along the winding narrow roads over mountain ridges and through lush valleys. Extravagantly-colored tropical flowers accenting the landscape were the kind of flora she had never seen along roads of the American mainland.

Crewe informed the local paper that she planned to see the Blue Hole Mineral Spring prior to leaving the island for another stop in Cuba. She also noted that she had put 6,500 miles on her motorcycle thus far.

After leaving Kingston, Crewe rode to Port Antonio. In that vicinity she had a minor collision with a car, which resulted in her spending a night at the Baptist Mission House. The next day she continued her trip to Port Antonio, both she and her Harley-Davidson apparently no worse for the incident.

After an obviously delightful time in Jamaica, Crewe sailed to Puerto Rico, landing at San Juan. She then explored the areas around the cities of Guanica and Fijardo. She was greatly impressed by the island's enormous sugar production, noting that she saw the major sugar mill at Guanica and the world's largest sugar plantation at Fijardo.

Puerto Rico obviously made a positive impression on Crewe, and she waxed poetic about its charms. "Porto Rico," she said in a *Texaco Star* story, "presents a mercurial spirit quite American. Its diffused mingling of flowers, coffee, fruits, and vegetation everywhere, with perfect roads, fills one with inspiring memories."

Crewe's stated plans called for another stop at Cuba upon leaving Puerto Rico, this time landing on the southeast corner of the island at the port of Santiago de Cuba. After seeing that part of Cuba, she made the short sail to the Isle of Pines off the island's south coast. She then went to Nassau for a stay of unknown length, and sailed next to Tampa, Florida, where she resumed her transcontinental travels.

TAMPA SERVED as the southern terminus of developer and business-man Henry B. Plant's Florida railroad network, as well as home port for a line of steamships sailing between there and Cuba. Though still a small city in 1915, it was a rapidly growing and strategically important area because of these transportation links. Miss Crewe would prob-ably have been amazed at the sight of the huge Tampa Hotel. Built by Henry Plant to serve winter visitors to Florida, the hotel was a Moor-ish architectural style, and its minarets loomed above the city's small buildings and palm trees.

Henry Plant was a major booster of Florida tourism, and he was convinced that the forests and swamps of the state would in time become home to thriving cities and a modern network of railroads and highways. Like Carl Fisher, Henry Flagler, and other early land developers, Plant saw the potential of Florida as a tourist destination and a winter home for weary northerners while most people saw only swamps, bugs, and sand.

Crewe's portrayal of the difficulties of motorcycling north on the terrible sandy and swampy roads between Tampa and Atlanta presents a stark picture and allows one to appreciate the tremendous changes that occurred over the following two decades. In large part, she would have followed the route of the future Dixie Highway.

Carl Fisher, in addition to his Florida developments, was also the original driving force behind the Lincoln Highway and the Dixie Highway. In 1914 he proposed a road connecting northern cities with Florida beaches, which would, coincidentally, carry tourists and new residents to his development—a place called Miami Beach.

By the summer of 1915 the highway's alignment was mapped out on paper, but it was too early for Crewe to have benefitted from any on-ground improvements to the road. What was to become the main road carrying those seeking to escape from Chicago and Detroit's winter cold to the sunny beaches of Florida was still an unimproved sandy trail when she bounced along its bumpy surface and powered her way through water-covered portions of the route. A Florida Good Roads Association representative told her that one day Florida would have an excellent road system, but that was only a hope and a dream in 1915.

From Atlanta Crewe traveled to Greenville and Spartanburg, South Carolina; then on to Charlotte, North Carolina; Washington D.C.; Baltimore, Philadelphia, and Atlantic City on her way back to New York City. Very little record now exists of exactly where she went on her way north beyond passing through these major cities, but excursions to see the area's historical sites and geology seem likely.

One of the places at which she stopped was the former site of Fort Runyon in Arlington, Virginia. The fort, built in the earliest days of the Civil War as part of the defense of Washington, D.C., was unusual in two ways—its large size and its pentagonal shape. In 1915 virtually nothing of the fort remained, but Crewe took a picture of the site, with its commanding view of the city. Thirty years later, the Pentagon was built very near to where Fort Runyon, and a charming visitor from Waco, had once stood.

ONCE BACK IN New York, Della Crewe's trail grows cold. At various times she mentioned that, after her island hopping trip, she intended to follow the Lincoln Highway west to San Francisco to the Panama-Pacific Exposition. That is, if she were still unable to sail to Europe. By the summer of 1915 the European war had grown into a monstrous affair that showed no signs of ending. It's possible, though unconfirmed, that she followed through with those cross-country plans.

In 1915, finally back home in Waco well over a year after she departed on the trip, Della reported that she had ridden a total of 10,778 miles on her epic journey. When the distance for a New York to San Francisco leg is added to the mileage she had accrued upon returning to New York from the Caribbean, it comes tantalizingly close to the nearly 11,000 mile total she had previously calculated. It might be that Della simply took one of her trademark long and circuitous routs back to Waco from New York City.

Any thought of sailing to Asia to journey through the Orient, however, received a major blow when Japan declared war on Germany in August 1914. As a result of Japan's action, hostilities spread to the western Pacific and China. Japanese planes bombed sites in China, and her navy prowled the Pacific seeking ships that might have a military or economic connection with Germany. Under such circumstances, an around-the-world trip would have been impossible regardless of the route.

With no end to the conflicts in sight, and in fact with the scope and ferocity of the war only getting steadily worse, Della had to call off plans to ride her motorcycle completely around the globe. Upon completing her 1914-15 journey, Crewe told reporters that she might make a cross-country trip on the Lincoln Highway in 1916. However, I've found no record of it.

Miss Crewe, perhaps with childhood memories of cold Midwestern winters, and recalling her frigid motorcycle ride across the country through the bitter November and December snows of 1914, moved to the Los Angeles area circa 1920. The paper trail for her disappears after 1926, but one can hope and imagine that she continued her marvelous experiences and kept riding her much-loved motorcycle under the warm southern California sun.

It's hard to think of Della living as a sedentary suburbanite satisfied with life in burgeoning Los Angeles. It is easier to imagine her on a bike, or behind the wheel of a car, heading off on wonderful adventures, wandering the country with a never-ending look of awe in her eyes and a ready smile on her face. A positive attitude and expansive world view such as hers would not be easily abandoned.

State-of-the-art highway signage in America circa 1915. (Photo used with permission of the University of Michigan Bentley Library)

The Great Adventure of Effie
and Avis Hotchkiss

—⊙∕∕⊙—

Pack up your troubles in your old kit bag and smile, smile, smile.
Don't let your joy and laughter hear the snag smile boys, that's the style
What's the use of worrying it never was worthwhile
So, pack up your troubles in your old kit bag and smile, smile, smile.[1]

Is it possible that Fred and Avis Hotchkiss had "effervescent" in mind in 1889 when they endowed their second daughter with the name Effie? Time would have proven them correct if this prophetic thought did influence the name they chose. As she grew from a gregarious tomboy to a woman for whom no challenge was too large and who was certain to find humor and humanity in every situation, her marvelous personality could be best described by the word effervescent.

Effie Hotchkiss was one of those rare people who possessed an ideal personality—an amalgam of optimism, happiness, intelligence, wit, and a can-do spirit—that causes people like her to rise above any situation they encounter. Add courage, confidence, resourcefulness, and fearlessness to this mix, and a truly unique individual is the outcome.

Her father might have unconsciously influenced her upbringing in a way that formed the daring and resourceful woman she ultimately became. Effie's mother said that Mr. Hotchkiss was not at all happy to have another daughter as his second child when he wanted a son so badly.

---

[1] Lyrics by George and Felix Powell, published by Chappell & Co. London, 1915

92

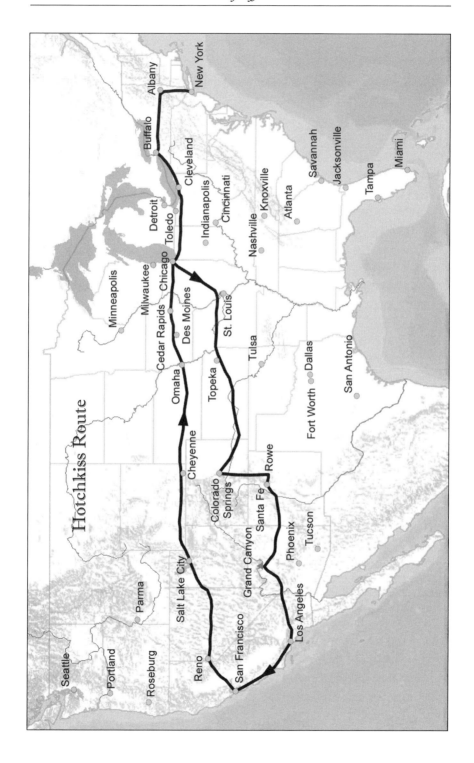

In a reflective mood, he eventually accepted reality and said that, as long as she was not a son, he hoped she would be "a rather devilish girl." If by "devilish" he meant full of life and mischief, he definitely got his wish!

Effie was certainly an exceptional person. She loved life and was loved by those who knew her, but the story of her fascinating life came close to being lost to future generations. Details would have died with her were it not for her two surviving accounts: an article she wrote for the *New York Sun* newspaper in the fall of 1915, and a journal she wrote decades later chronicling her life story. We are fortunate indeed that these two documents exist, enabling us to know and appreciate at least some of the details of her remarkable story.

Mr. Hotchkiss' wish for a son was fulfilled in 1893 when Effie's brother Everett was born. While the children were still young, Fred bought a farm in Durham Township of Greene County, in the beautiful Catskill Mountains of New York. According to Effie, he intended to live there in an effort to regain his health. Fred died at his farm shortly after 1900.

Although the rest of the Hotchkiss family was still living in Brooklyn, Fred was buried at a small cemetery in the Catskills. The entire family was there for the funeral services, and when Effie was told that she could spend the whole summer at the farm, she was thrilled. She immediately decided that the men at the local firehouse in Brooklyn were going to have to do without the chocolate cakes that she delivered to them every day. They had taken her under their wing to, in her words, help her mother "with the difficult job of making a lady of me."

Effie's love of farming and of the out-of-doors was born and nurtured that summer. Her holiday at the farm was a delightful experience filled with rambunctious high-jinks as she and Bill, son of the family overseeing the farm, roamed the hills, fields, and forests of the beautiful region. They got on the wrong end of a trapped skunk and nearly drowned while fishing for trout in a pool below a waterfall. She tried to help with the various chores around the farm, but succeeded only in causing much more work for 22-year old George, the bachelor hired hand.

She and Bill surreptitiously arranged a raffle, with George as the prize husband for the woman holding the winning ticket, all in an attempt to get him married so he that could enjoy the marital bliss they were certain he desired. Perhaps worst of all for poor George, they got into his hidden stash of hard cider, leaving the spigot open as they stumbled away and causing the remainder of the precious liquid to drain onto the ground. These were but a few of the intrigues and shenanigans that filled their days.

UNFORTUNATELY FOR EFFIE, the adults in her life felt that her safety and Bill's, as well as the smooth operation of the farm, would be enhanced if she moved back to the city. In the strange workings of fate, this proved to be a positive event because, when walking the family dog on the streets of New York City a short time later, she saw five motorcycles roar by and she fell in love again. She decided that she would save every penny and that, upon turning sixteen, she would buy her very own motorcycle.

The years passed, no doubt filled with all the drama that one can imagine for a teenaged Effie, and she eventually bought her first motorcycle. The best she could afford was a well-used machine with no frills. It was a Marsh-Metz and was powered by a 4-horsepower V-twin 1,000 cc engine. The old Marsh-Metz, called MM by owners, was a bare bones model. As Effie described it, the machine was "starterless, headlight less, and a lot of other lesses."

People who wished to ride this machine first pushed it as fast as they could and then jumped on at the engine's first sputtering. Effie's first endeavor to ride her machine didn't go well. After she failed in several attempts to get it running, her brother Everett came to the rescue and pushed while she sat on the bike. As she described it:

> "The engine spit and sputtered, I turned the gas and spark on full force, lost control of the machine, bounced across the sidewalk and ended half way up a flight of steps of an English basement house. A little more practice and I might have made it all the way up and rung the bell."

The MM lasted only a week in Effie's aggressive hands, and she began looking for a replacement. She found it in another used machine, this time an early model single cylinder Harley-Davidson being sold by "a blue eyed, dark haired Irishman" named Ted. Effie decided then and there that she was interested in both the machine and the owner. To her delight, Ted offered to bring the motorcycle to her house the following Saturday and take her for a test ride. When the weekend arrived, weather conditions were perfect. Effie left her mother with the impression that they'd be gone an hour or two.

They rode to the ocean and sat talking about motorcycles and what Effie described as "other less important things" for much longer than they had intended. On the way home, they had a flat tire and no means to repair it. So they spent a couple hours pushing the bike to a garage where they left it, and then made the long walk to Effie's house.

Her mother was convinced that any number of unthinkably terrible things had happened to Effie and raised quite a scene when they finally arrived home. Effie thought that perhaps that was not the best time to introduce Ted to the family. She just couldn't understand all the fuss. As she wrote:

> "Go out for a ride and come home dripping blood all over the place and no one pays very much attention, go out for a ride, have a good time and come home all in one piece and there was the devil to pay. What a zany family!"

Despite the less than auspicious circumstances of their first meeting, Effie bought the bike and took weekly rides with Ted and his friends, who had all moved up to larger and faster cycles. Effie's underpowered machine had trouble keeping up with the more powerful twin-cylindered models, which prompted her to buy her third motorcycle. She called the day that she took possession of her new bike— a twin cylinder fresh off the assembly line—"probably the proudest moment of my life." According to her granddaughter, the new machine of which Effie was so proud was an Indian.

Shortly after purchasing the bike, Effie came close to committing her first and only homicide. She came home one day to find a friend of her brother's in their garage, with Indian parts spread far and wide across the floor. It seems the friend got bored while waiting for her brother Everett to get home, so he decided to see what made the Indian tick. Under threat of dire consequences, he quickly reassembled the bike and was *persona non grata* at Effie's house after that.

It was also at this time that handsome, dark-haired Ted suggested that they elope. Effie thought it was a grand idea, and they hatched a plan to ride up to the farm the following Saturday to inform family and friends. The night before their planned departure, Ted's motorcycle was stolen, so they decided to ride together on Effie's bike. The trip from New York City to the Catskills on rough rocky roads and traversing many hills proved to be more than her bike could accommodate with two riders. After a long, grueling day of flat tires and mechanical break-downs, they decided that perhaps divine intervention was trying to tell them something. If elopement were this much trouble, Effie rational-ized, marriage would surely be "too awful to contemplate."

WITH MARRIAGE PLANS OFF, Effie turned to those duties and activi-ties that life places on every person's plate. She got a job as a clerk in a Wall Street financial center and, as she rode the train to work each day, dreamed of green fields and of a time when she could forget clocks and calendars. As she later reflected:

> "I started bravely. I was ambitious, enthusiastic, eager to accom-plish something. But, little by little, I realized how futile ambi-tion is when one is just part of a great machine. Years rolled by in nothing but monotony. And always I dreamed of those fields. The country with its rivers, mountains and valleys spread out before my mind. It goaded me almost beyond endurance."

A visit to a doctor gave her an opening. He advised taking a break from her job. She decided she would follow his suggestion and, while not working, would further explore the world on a motorcycle. With income from her job and some inheritance money, Effie paid $310 for a new 1915 Harley-Davidson. This latest example of two-wheeled splendor was a model 11-J with a 61-cid V-twin engine that produced 11 horsepower. It was a major step up from the first two machines she had owned, and more capable than the smaller Indian.

It had a manual kick starter, though improved from what had been used in prior models. 1915 marked the first use of what was called a "step starter." This system used what resembled bicycle pedals which the operator pushed to turn over the engine.

It had a three speed transmission with a claimed ability to handle a 60 percent grade. Suspension was crude, with springs under the large bicycle-style seat providing most of the barrier between rough roads and the rider. Footboards provided a comfortable place for a rider to place his or her feet while under way. Braking was accomplished by means of a coaster brake on the rear hub—the same technology that was utilized on bicycles for decades. The final drive was by way of a chain to the rear wheel, and large fenders with mud flaps, a sign of the time, completed the picture.

The 28-inch wheels on this and most motorcycles of that period meant that they were tall and required special care when getting on and off the machine or when at a standstill. Modern bikes have wheels in the 17–21 inch diameter range, and most have a 26–30-inch seat height. This difference allows for significantly lower centers of gravity for the various models and for easier handling, especially for shorter persons.

With some time off work, a bit of inheritance money at her disposal and a new motorcycle, Effie decided to pursue an ambitious dream. Without so much as a second thought, she made plans to undertake something that had never been done before.

The reasons that nobody had accomplished what Effie set out to do in the summer of 1915 were many and they were significant. You see, she decided to ride from New York to San Francisco on her motorcycle and return to the East Coast via a different route, more than doubling the number of miles that other cross-country travelers had accumulated in previous excursions. What's more, Effie took the idea to yet another level and attached a sidecar to her motorcycle.

According to the *New York Sun* article, Effie purchased the sidecar because her mother wished to go for local rides. In her journal many years later, she wrote that she purchased the sidecar after she decided to go to California so that she could take her mother along on this history-making five month journey!

It would seem that the 1915 article is more accurate, not only because of its timeliness, but because other facts tend to bear it out. Effie's article in the Sun made it clear that her mother was an active partner in conceiving the idea of the trip.

To put things in context, note that Avis Hotchkiss weighed 215 pounds. This required some alterations on the sidecar to beef up the suspension. Even more to the point, bear in mind that for the entire nearly 9,000 miles of their trip, this weight increased the challenges of handling a rig through deep mud, sand, loose gravel, and steep mountain roadways. It was a challenge just to operate a motorcycle on the roads that they encountered, let alone managing hundreds of pounds of additional weight. That Effie was able to pull it off is beyond amazing.

When Effie told her employer and co-workers that she was taking an extended leave to go to California on a motorcycle, they were stunned. "You are crazy. The thing is suicidal. It will kill your mother. You simply don't realize what you are undertaking." These were just some of the comments she received from understandably concerned friends and co-workers. To the assertion that she didn't know what she was getting into, Effie responded with "Probably not" but went on to declare that "My horizon has been very limited. Now I am going to broaden it."

Effie's mother provides more background as to her daughter's personality and desire for adventure. As reported in the *Middletown Daily Times-Press*, Avis said:

> "Dolls and needlework never appealed to Miss Effie, but baseball and like pastimes just suited her fancy. She hopes to establish a record and to convince other girls that motorcycling is a healthy sport for women. In pure love of the sport, Effie hopes to arouse an interest in it among women."

Avis went on to say:

> "Fear doesn't bother me. I can safely trust my daughter and I am looking forward to an enjoyable trip. I do not fear breakdowns for Effie, besides being a most careful driver is a good mechanic and does her own repairing with her own tools."

Clearly Effie had earned the full respect and support of her mother, despite youthful shenanigans that had surely tested Avis Hotchkiss's patience to the maximum.

Of the female motorcyclists portrayed in this book, Effie was the only one who wanted to include a firearm with her equipment and supplies. This was probably due to the fact that she was comfortable with firearms and had been around them on the farm, as opposed to believing that she had a critical need to have it for safety's sake. As she said with her usual humor and wit, "I had always wanted one but never had a good reason for it. The only wild animals I had known were the bulls and bears of Wall Street and an occasional drug store wolf."

In pursuit of a pistol, she went to a local sporting goods store and browsed the options, hiding her complete ignorance of handguns. Only after she made her selection did she learn from the clerk that New York required a permit to purchase the weapon. Seeing the look of disappointment on her face, the clerk told her that New Jersey's firearm purchase law was much more relaxed. As she later wrote:

> "He told me that the State of New Jersey did not seem to care who shot whom as long as it was done in good clean fun and a permit to carry a gun was not required in that state. My sister had a friend who lived in New Jersey and, while she did not know it, she was about to acquire a gun."

Sometime later, at a party in New Jersey, the friend mentioned that the handgun was ready to be picked up. A newspaper reporter was attending the same party and overheard her mention that she had bought a pistol. He was curious as to why she needed one and inquired, so she informed him of her plans for a transcontinental trip. His resulting story, the only article published before their upcoming journey, appeared about two weeks prior to her departure, and a small number of other papers picked it up.

Newspaper and magazine reporters did not follow the Hotchkiss transcontinental round-trip tour as closely as they had Della Crewe's around-the-globe attempt and the Van Buren trip a year later. Libraries, museums, and newspaper archives, therefore, have far fewer articles and other documentation about the Hotchkiss trip than for Della Crewe's and the Van Buren sisters' journeys.

Several reasons for this come to mind. First, Crewe's tour drew notice because it involved a woman's unprecedented solo trip around the world on a motorcycle; an outrageously bold and daring effort.

Having it impacted to the degree that it was by the war in Europe only added to the drama and thus to the interest shown by newspapers across the country.

Also, with every passing year, cross-country trips, albeit usually in cars, were becoming more routine and less newsworthy. The Van Buren sisters' trip received much coverage because they were on a widely-publicized mission for the National Preparedness Movement and to convince the Army that women could serve as military dispatch riders. The sisters were also active in the New York motorcycling community, and leading motorcycle journals of the day thought their trip merited additional coverage.

The lesser amount of newspaper coverage for Effie and Avis was also because they wanted to make the trip for personal reasons, not for publicity, fame, or a cause. Effie did it to satisfy her personal desire for adventure, excitement, to see the West, and because it was a reflection of the person she was—a free spirit to whom open spaces and the open road beckoned. She also wanted to go on the ambitious journey because she loved riding motorcycles and wanted to take the ultimate trip.

Effie and Avis also had no corporate support or financial backing for their adventure. Corporate backing, common in that era for trips such as this one, provided financial and logistical help, perhaps even a vehicle, and publicity, too. Sponsors would also have ensured that the press was made aware of the trip's progress all along the way and that newspaper reporters were on hand to write positive accounts of the vehicle and driver as they made their way across the continent.

Finally, world events overshadowed Effie's trip. Just two days before she and her mother departed, the RMS *Lusitania*—one of the most modern passenger ships in the world—set sail from New York, bound for England. Four days after the Hotchkisses left New York a German U-Boat sank the ship, with a horrendous loss of life. Of the more than 1,000 people who died, 114 were Americans.

This event made the headlines of newspapers across the country for many days. Because trans-oceanic travel on a ship such as the *Lusitania* was so costly, many of the passengers were well- known figures from the world of high society, politics, industry, or entertainment. Americans suddenly had little time to consider the activities of recreational travelers as they vehemently argued about going to war.

Even when under way, the Hotchkisses did not go out of their way to publicize their trip by meeting with local officials or reporters as many others did. Finally, unlike many other trekkers, Effie and her mother did not spend their nights at hotels. They either camped along the road or they sought a room at facilities such as repair garages, ranch houses and other out-of-the-way places. This meant that they did not attract the attention that drivers normally did as they came into small towns or villages looking for lodging. As a result, we have few small town newspaper accounts of their progress.

ACCORDING TO EFFIE'S *Sun* article, the grand journey had departed Leffert's Park in Brooklyn early on Monday, May 3, 1915. Effie displayed a banner emblazoned with Bushwick MC—the name of her local motorcycle club—to serve as a talisman and reminder of their Brooklyn home.

With the exception of Effie's leather boots and gloves, the Hotchkiss women did not wear gear designed for motorcycling. Rather than the common leather helmet and goggles, each wore a cloth cap with a bill designed to keep the sun out of her eyes. Their slacks and long coats were of a heavy cloth material. They stowed rain gear, which they used frequently, in the sidecar.

Effie was 26 when they departed, although newspaper stories of the time reported her age in various articles as 20 or 22 years old. With her 51-year-old mother securely ensconced in the sidecar, Effie went by way of the most common route that New Yorkers used when going westward: north to Albany and then across the Mohawk Valley to Buffalo. As Effie put it in the *New York Sun* article, "Friends went along as far as Ossining, New York, and both of us were nervous, tearful and frightened when they left us and we realized we were alone, face to face with the great unknown world."

GOING NORTH TO Albany and then west may seem out of the way for travelers from New York City, but it really was, by far, the best way to go. Roads going through the highlands of New Jersey and especially through the mountains of Pennsylvania were at times impassable or treacherous, and difficult in the best weather. Running perpendicular to the Alleghenies as they did, the trails over the mountains were narrow and steep, with precipitous drop-offs.

In contrast to Pennsylvania roads, the Post Road along the Hudson River's east side was a well-maintained, heavily-used thoroughfare with necessary services along the way. The road from Albany to Buffalo was also a well-traveled and improved primary dirt road. For the most part, journeying from New York City to Buffalo was commonplace and unchallenging, as long as recent weather conditions hadn't been too severe.

The Mohawk Valley route had been the preferred way of going west from New York City since the first "long distance" automobile trips began in the 1890s. The first cross-country automobile journey—Dr. H. Nelson Jackson's 1903 trip from the Pacific to the Atlantic coast in a Winton motor carriage—used the Mohawk Valley route across the state of New York in his final approach to New York City.

THE HOTCHKISSES encountered no serious problems and rode all the way to Cleveland without incident. They were with friends on a week-long stopover there when they read the newspaper accounts of the *Lusitania*, and it no doubt cast a pall on their trip for several days. But they proceeded west across Ohio, Indiana, and Illinois to Chicago. This was Effie's first trip to this region of the country, and they apparently spent a considerable amount of time exploring the Great Lakes shoreline and other regional attractions.

Effie and her mother rarely stayed in hotels. They probably had several reasons for this, though Effie specifically mentioned only one. She wrote that they felt guilty staying in a hotel because she and her mother were always so dirty. They undoubtedly had other reasons, one of which would have been saving money, especially on a trip without corporate sponsorship. Spending five months' worth of nights in hotels would have been prohibitively expensive.

Also, they both made it clear from the beginning that they intended to "sleep in the open" as much as possible. It is obvious that they made this choice because they enjoyed the freedom and adventure of camping. They packed a tent and necessary camping gear in the sidecar.

When not camping, they sought out spare rooms at garages or homes. One night, a local constable opened a barber shop so that they could sleep in the barber chairs when they could find no room elsewhere in town and the motorcycle was at the local blacksmith shop being repaired.

Effie noted that she had to visit at least one blacksmith in each state she rode through to repair the inevitable damage to the cycle or sidecar that resulted from the rough roads. Looking back, a person can only marvel at the skill of turn-of-the-century blacksmiths who, with only a forge and relatively crude tools, could fabricate intricate metal pieces to replace or repair parts made in the most up-to-date factories.

It was in an Indiana garage owner's spare room that Avis Hotchkiss learned a hobby from the owner's wife which, for the next five months, would drive Effie to distraction. That pastime was tatting. As she confided to her journal years later:

> "To this day the sight of a tatting shuttle, empty or loaded, makes me gag. If I stopped the machine for a minute, regardless of why, mother tatted even though the stop might mean I needed a wrench or some kindred tool for repairs. There she would sit, firmly ensconced on the tool box, busily tatting. Did she dig out the tools for me or even remove herself so I could get to them? Oh, no, she just tatted. When I would firmly demand access to my tool box she would dreamily remove herself, wander over to the side of the road, sit down and tat. I loved my mother very much but was often tempted to commit mayhem with that tatting shuttle."

As the rains began to fall and the going got rough, her mother's tendency to tat calmly while things were spinning out of control drove Effie to the edge. As she later recorded:

> "A resurrected Noah dashing by in his ark would not have been too surprising. The motorcycle learned to swim and I, who could not, wondered if life preservers could be purchased this far inland. I suppose, if it came to a pinch, mother, being

Avis patiently waits, tatting shuttle in her lap, while a blacksmith performs necessary repairs on their motorcycle and sidecar. (Used with permission of the Hotchkiss Family Estate)

an excellent swimmer, would rescue me. Of course she might be too busy with her tatting to bother and I had visions of her snagging a passing chicken coop, sailing down the stream on it and all the time busily tatting."

East of Chicago, the main roads were generally in at least fair shape, and in dry weather one could count on the dirt or gravel surface to be passable, albeit dusty. If it had rained recently, then even the well-maintained eastern roads would quickly turn slippery and muddy, making riding a suddenly difficult and even dangerous business.

Traveling on eastern roads ensured that one would regularly encounter repair garages and gasoline supplies. Also, if a machine broke down on the road, help would arrive soon. West of Chicago, roads became less reliable and services sparser.

Daughter and mother spent a few days seeing the sights of Chicago, having their picture taken to mark the occasion, and then rode southwest across Illinois to St. Louis. They traversed Illinois on

Effie and Avis Hotchkiss in Chicago on their way west. Beyond Chicago their journey became much more difficult.

a dirt road called the Pontiac Trail, significant portions of which would become U.S. Route 66 just a decade later.

They were thrilled crossing the Mississippi River on the McKinley Bridge, and Avis even put her tatting aside to take in the marvelous view from 90 feet above the mighty Mississippi. The high, steel truss bridge built in 1910 continued to carry Route 66 traffic across the river until 1930, when the higher-capacity Chain of Rocks Bridge was built nearby.

Continuing west across the sparsely populated Missouri countryside to Kansas City, their trials and tribulations began in earnest. In most years, Spring and early Summer are periods of much rain throughout the Midwest, and 1915 proved to be an exceptionally wet year. The sodden conditions made it extremely difficult for Effie as she slipped and slid along those nearly impassable paths. She often had to extricate her machine from deep mud by whatever means possible.

Roads had turned into deep gumbo mud, rivers had overflowed their banks, and bridges were washed out. Effie wrote:

> "Missouri was probably no wetter than any other state but I swear it had stickier mud. I had driven in other states with the water gently lapping over my feet but in Missouri the mud covered them. The stuff would actually roil up off the dry ground under it after a rain storm and riding up hill was like trying to make time on a treadmill, you just did not get anyplace. One exceptionally dreary, drizzly day we met three hills in rapid succession, all of them the same degree of stickiness. Mother had become so discouraged she had even abandoned her tatting."

That already difficult day was going to get much worse before it ended. They came to a bridge that someone had torn out. The local road department had intentions to replace the demolished bridge with a new one, but hadn't gotten around to building it yet. As Effie described it,

> "I could not persuade the motorcycle to leap over the gap so tried going around it. We ended up like a lonesome fly on sticky paper, stuck fast and no one there to help us. My sense of humor had been rained on once too often to bear up under this latest annoyance and when I double damned the road commissioners and hoped they ended up building roads in hell mother was too tired to even say "Why Effie!" I found some old fence posts, or I should say I fell over them in the dark. I pried and prayed that machine back on the road and then found some moth eaten planks and built a bridge. We finally made the next town and a couple of rather lumpy beds."

It is easy to visualize these two women, covered head to toe in their mud-splattered rain gear, slowly making their lonely way down dark and gloomy, muddy trails in the pouring rain. It is harder to imagine what they thought as they endured conditions that would have caused virtually any other person to abandon the trip, saying that they had given it their best shot, but that conditions were just impossibly difficult. Effie and Avis gave no indication that they ever had thoughts about turning back or abandoning their quest. They proceeded onward with single-minded determination regardless of the difficulties they encountered.

At one particularly bad river crossing in the Midwest, which proved impossible without a long detour, they convinced a crew of railroad workers to load their rig on a flatcar and transport it across the flooded stream on the rail bridge. Effie had several positive encounters with rail workers and she counted them among her favorite people.

Struggling to keep her vehicle on the narrow, muddy trails through fields of stunted corn yellowed from too much rain, Effie may well have sympathized with the farmers whose crops were dying. She knew that their tenuous grip on financial survival was slipping away with every new rainfall. She was just passing through; they had to survive for the long term. As she described it, "We saw more water than anything else, roads were under water, bridges washed out, and it rained constantly. Corn had been planted three times and each time rotted in the ground. Our ponchos were worth their weight in gold."

From western Missouri to Santa Fe, Effie followed one of the few routes that crossed the continent—the Trail to Sunset/National Old Trails Road. This road largely followed the Santa Fe Trail on which settlers had made their way west on horseback just two generations earlier.

The trail began in Independence, Missouri, and went through Hutchinson and Dodge City, Kansas. Near Dodge City, the Santa Fe Trail diverged into northern and southern roads. The northern, or Mountain Trail, followed the Arkansas River to Pueblo, Colorado, and other Colorado towns and forts before turning south. The southern branch, called the Cimarron Trail, angled southwest from Dodge City, following the Cimarron River for a short stretch, and rejoined the Mountain Trail east of Santa Fe, New Mexico. From there the Trail to Sunset continued across Arizona and through the Mojave Desert, eventually making its way to the coast.

Effie followed the Mountain route to Colorado Springs, Colorado. Although she did not document which, if any, of the local attractions they visited, it is easy to imagine their seeing nearby sights such as Seven Falls, Garden of the Gods, and the Manitou Cliff Dwellings.

From Colorado Springs they drove south into New Mexico to rejoin the National Old Trails Road, which barely qualified to be called a road; it was more of a two-track trail. Ahead of them lay a vast wilderness. Having reached the necessary population base to qualify for statehood only three years earlier, New Mexico and Arizona were enormous, mostly unpopulated states little changed from the frontier days of just one generation earlier. Towns were few with great distances between them.

INDEPENDENCE DAY found the New Yorkers camping on a New Mexico mountain in temperatures low enough to form frost on their blankets. Greeted by the sunrise breaking over the mountains, Effie woke her mother, saying "Wake up, mother. We've arrived at last in God's own country, and Wall Street is just a nightmare of the past."

Imagine the aroma of coffee, being warmed over a campfire, floating in the still mountain air. Hear the sounds and picture the sights of morning dawning in the vast openness that surrounded them. Violet rays of the rising sun, dim and without warmth at that early hour, illuminated immutable mountains and mesas as far as the women could see, leaving them in awe. That place, and the sensory delights that they enjoyed, made all the rough miles they endured worthwhile. It was a scene powerful enough to change a person's life. On that beautiful mountain top, they were truly about as far from city life as one could get. Effie's love of the West may have been shaped forever in her mind and heart on that memorable morning.

AT ANOTHER mountain campsite the circumstances were dramatically different. An incident occurred there that could have turned disastrous very quickly and caused the end of their trip, if not worse. It was early morning, and breakfast and a pot of coffee were slowly warming on a sputtering campfire.

"The wood was damp and merely smoldered and I was busy at some minor repairs and asked mother to pep up the fire, expecting her to use a little squirt gun attached to the cap of the gasoline tank. Mother is not the type that does things in a small way. She picked up a gallon of gas I carried for emergency and stood over the fire dribbling a little stream of gas on it. She really got quick action. There was an immediate response and the entire can of gasoline as well as our breakfast burst into flame.

"Mother was too petrified to let go of the can until I yelled at her to toss it away and she did—right at me. My cap, sweater, breeches and boots joined the conflagration. Luckily my hair was well tucked under my cap and the peak of it protected my eyes. I got my sweater and cap off and the flames beat out on my breeches and boots before being more than a rather rare roast when we both could have been so well done. The can of gas did not explode but it was heart breaking to see those potential miles of driving going up in flame. And we never did get our coffee."

Effie rarely had an opportunity to just relax and enjoy the ride. When she wasn't on 100 percent alert because of road conditions and hidden dangers, she had other problems to solve. It was in the wilderness southeast of Santa Fe that her resourcefulness came in especially handy.

Suffering a flat tire caused by a puncture in the inner tube, and having no spare tubes left, Effie improvised. She took a blanket, shredded it, and stuffed it inside the tire. With this clever alternative to the pneumatic tire, they rode slowly to the town of Rowe, New Mexico, a small town along the Atchison, Topeka and Santa Fe railroad.

There they met three young men who were also on their way to San Francisco for the Panama-Pacific Exposition. The gallant fellows were only too happy to help Effie in her predicament and agreed to go with her on the train for the 30-mile trip to Santa Fe to locate a replacement inner tube. Giving her pistol to Avis for protection, Effie left mother and motorcycle parked near the tracks in Rowe. It is all too easy to imagine the apprehension the women shared as they parted company in the New Mexico outback. Rowe might be a bit larger today, but it is still little more than a collection of small homes and closed shops. The railroad still runs through the village but the depot that was once a connection to the outside world has long since vanished.

WITH HER CHIVALROUS helpers always close at hand, Effie got on the next passing train and rode it to Santa Fe. After much searching, she finally found a man who had a used tube, with five patches already on it, and who agreed to sell it at the price of a new one. Effie said that he cheated himself. She would have paid twice as much!

Effie and companions got back to the depot just in time to see the train rolling down the tracks toward Rowe; she had missed it and had no way of getting word to her mother. There would not be another train until the next morning.

Always the cheerful person, ready to make the best of whatever life threw at her, Effie enjoyed a meal and moonlight walk with her eager suitors. Her night on the town wasn't without a cost, however. She was very worried about her mother, left as she was with no food, water, or shelter. She wrote:

> "I could not sleep all night for wondering how I would dispose of mother's body. Would I bury her where she lay or ship her home? The boys and I went to breakfast together and then to the train, with promises to meet again in San Francisco and give romance a little better break. As the train pulled into Rowe I saw mother peacefully sitting in the side car, very much alive and busily tatting."

When her mother asked what she had brought her to eat, Effie realized that she had been so worried about her mother starving to death that she had forgotten to bring her any food!

Avis did not have need for the pistol left behind for her protection. I think anyone who encountered her could tell she was a woman who was not to be taken lightly, whether armed with a pistol or tatting needles.

UPON LEAVING THE WET middle section of the country behind, the Hotchkiss women confronted new difficulties. Roads in the prairies had, at least, been fairly recognizable, but they turned into difficult traces across the deserts and barren rocky landscapes of the Southwest.

Mountainous terrain also presented new challenges to Effie. As skilled as she was, her experience thus far had not prepared her for mountain riding. The La Bajada escarpment near Santa Fe in particular could have caused our bold adventurers to consider that perhaps they should plan a different route west, no matter the time lost.

The escarpment was well known to travelers going back hundreds of years when the Spanish first passed through the area. These early explorers assigned the steep hill its name, which translates to The Descent or The Drop in English. Between 1903 and 1909, laborers and convicts blasted a series of sharp switchbacks up the cliff face, opening a slow and tortuous, narrow path that was dangerous in the best of conditions. One miscalculated move meant falling hundreds of feet down the volcanic precipice.

Even after the road was further improved years later and designated as Route 66, travelers feared this stretch. Local residents earned spending money by driving the cars of apprehensive tourists up or down the mountain. A sign at the top of the peak placed by the New Mexico Highway Department in the late 1920s offered little consolation to early drivers on the Mother Road. It read:

> *La Bajada Hill*
> *Warning*
> *Safe Speed 10 Miles*
> *Watch Sharp Curves*
> *This road is not fool proof*
> *But safe for a sane driver*
> *Use Low Gear*

Effie would have kept the bike in first gear to maintain control of the motorcycle, sidecar, and hundreds of pounds of weight as they worked their way down through the hairpin curves. This was a place where she hoped to not meet any other vehicles—usually a desirable event on the lonely roads of the day—so they could stay as far as possible from the sheer drops along the edge of the narrow roadway. Perhaps Avis tatted with a special intensity during the adventure to keep from looking at the yawning void just a few feet away.

Today, vehicles on Interstate 25 easily make the transition to and from the Rio Grande Valley and the summit of the volcanic plateau, barely noticing the geologic obstacle that once represented a daunting barrier to travelers.

ONE OF THE MORE fortunate realities about travel in this era was that the main east–west automobile routes often ran near or even adjacent to railroad tracks. The earliest explorers had long ago discovered the best routes across the prairies and through the mountains. Wagon trains then followed those early paths, and railroads later followed these same natural routes.

A rail line paralleled some of the route that Effie rode across Kansas, New Mexico, and Arizona. Similarly, that portion of the Lincoln Highway across the prairies ran alongside the Union Pacific line for hundreds of miles. In these stretches of roadway, a person could flag down a train in an emergency. Trains also stopped at many of the small towns such as Rowe that had built up along the tracks.

BUT SIMPLY BEING near a railroad track wasn't enough to guarantee a trouble-free trip. After endless days of struggling through Midwestern mud, Effie was ecstatic upon reaching the dry firm ground of the Southwest. Here she could make her machine perform as it was meant to, and she could once again experience the exhilaration of motorcycling; the cool wind in her hair, the warm sun on her face and the joys of the open road as she glided effortlessly through a landscape that was as alien to her as Mars.

The going would now be easy, she thought. After all, nothing could be worse than mile after mile of deep gumbo mud that frustrated all attempts at forward progress. The dry air and higher elevation would be a welcome relief to the hot humid miasma of the middle of the continent.

Alas, it wasn't to be. The normally dry deserts of New Mexico and Arizona had their own unique hazards, silently and invisibly waiting for the next unsuspecting traveler. It was a common problem, reported by several people from that era, and the situation created major danger, but there was little a person could do beyond being very cautious. Ironically, even in the arid desert, the basis of this new peril was once again that old motorcycling nemesis—rain.

Sudden heavy rainstorms, "gully washers" as rural residents called them with good reason, caused channels to develop across trails and roads. These miniature gullies were often a foot or more deep, and hitting one suddenly was a sure way to cause major damage to a vehicle and its occupants. What made this condition especially treacherous was that these channels would often be filled with fine powdery windblown dust during dry periods, giving the appearance of a solid road surface. Washouts that extended across the dirt roads crisscrossing the nation a century ago were common and potentially deadly.

Alice Ramsey described one example in her book about her 1909 trip. Near Fish Springs, Utah, she came across a three-to-four-foot deep gully washed across the entire twelve-foot wide road! This type of hazard was common in those years and was but one reason why travel was slow and careful, undertaken only by those whose nerves matched the threats that lay in ambush for them. It also explains why only the most foolhardy attempted nighttime travel.

Effie was blissfully unaware of this new threat until one of these gullies materialized before her and Avis. As she described the incident;

"Dry roads caused even more damage than muddy roads. One day found us traveling over a wretched road at a snail's pace for mile after mile. After these boring miles, things began to look a little better. The road leveled up, I upped the speed and then we went up. In those happy days I did not chase the needle very far around the scale and consequently could fly through the air with the greatest of ease. A high flight makes for a heavy landing and, to my amazement and indignation, I woke up in a field with a crippled leg and found the motorcycle and fellow sufferer a far worse tragedy.

"When the fireworks in my head subsided I looked around for mother. She was too heavy to fly very far and there she sat bewailing the loss of her nose. Her nose was numb and the blood was flowing from it in a stream so she thought she had lost it. When I tried to get to her I found one of my legs had turned to rubber, although I could feel no broken bones. The only explanation was that the accident must have been caused by one wheel dropping in a dust filled rut I had not seen."

Effie's machine was badly damaged, and they were in the middle of nowhere. In fact, she was actually lost, as she had a propensity to be. By great luck, along came a car whose occupants were also lost. The passengers and Effie were able to twist and bend parts enough so that the bike and sidecar could, at least, go down the road. They had to go very slowly, however, because the machine now had no brakes, and the front fork was badly bent, making steering problematic.

As they worked their way tentatively toward the next small town, the unfortunate women found themselves on a hill with a sharp curve at the bottom. Without brakes and with greatly reduced steering abilities, Effie was unable to negotiate the curve and flew over the embankment at the base of the hill…right into a camp of Native Americans who were minding their own business. With more humor than most people could possibly have found at that point, Effie described the mayhem and shouting that ensued, as well as the additional injuries and damage suffered by machine and people alike. Despite having seen his wife hit by a flying motorcycle that appeared out of nowhere, one of the men helped Effie get the cycle and sidecar upright on its three unsteady wheels and rolling down the trail once more.

After her two serious accidents, Effie figuratively limped into the small town of Hackberry, Arizona, on her badly damaged motorcycle, with no brakes and extremely limited steering capability. Her mother literally limped the several miles into town, unwilling to face a possible third accident by riding in the sidecar attached to the badly damaged motorcycle.

The local blacksmith shook his head in amazement at the pile of damaged metal parts Effie brought into his small shop, but confirmed he could perform the needed repairs, a response that must have brightened an otherwise very trying and difficult day. Though he had never seen a motorcycle before, the blacksmith was true to his word. Putting all his skills and ingenuity to work, he had the machine back in running order the next day.

Although Effie makes no mention of it, one can guess that, after taking their motorcycle to the blacksmith for repairs, she and her mother made their way to the local doctor to have their many bruises and cuts addressed.

It was in Effie's description of the process of paying for the black-smith's services that she first raised the issue of money. It highlights the means by which tourists in the 1910s were able to travel without carrying large amounts of coin or paper money, as had been necessary just a few years earlier. Wealthy people in the 19th century could obtain Letters of Credit, which were honored by many distant and even foreign banks, but the average person normally had to carry gold or money. Of course, this was inconvenient and was also an invitation to be robbed, as it was well known that ordinary travelers would have large amounts of money hidden somewhere on their person.

Enter the concept of a "traveler's check." It wasn't until 1890, when banker J.C. Fargo grew frustrated with the inconvenience of using Letters of Credit while traveling, that things began to change. Being president of a large bank and associated with other financial services companies helped Mr. Fargo achieve his goal of a inventing a better financial mousetrap. His American Express Company came up with the solution. Beginning in 1891 American Express began offering what they called "traveler's cheques" in ten, twenty, fifty and one hundred dollar denominations. When American Express agreed to assume responsibility for fraudulent or forged checks, and to reimburse customers for lost checks, their product became widely used and accepted by banks across the nation and, ultimately, the world. Effie specifically mentioned her use of a traveler's check to pay for the blacksmith's services, so they apparently were carrying American Express checks.

The Hotchkisses benefited from improvements made to the National Old Trails Road, completed in the fall of 1914 that allowed a shorter route to California. Prior to the upgrades to this old Indian trail, travelers drove from Albuquerque southwest to Phoenix, then west to San Diego or Los Angeles. The National Old Trails Road made a straighter line west from Albuquerque to Holbrook and Flagstaff, Arizona, crossing the Colorado River at Needles, California.

This route was not only significantly shorter, it also put Effie and Avis in a position to see two famous landmarks—the Petrified Forest and the Grand Canyon. Effie left no record of what they thought of the Grand Canyon, but she did write that she was unimpressed with the Petrified Forest. She had apparently expected to see standing trees, not what she described as "a bunch of stones lying on the ground."

PERHAPS THE MOST challenging obstacle that lay in Effie and Avis's path was the Mojave Desert. Friends and co-workers in New York had warned them about the dangers of trying to cross this inhospitable territory, saying that it would be virtually impossible for the two of them to attempt it on a motorcycle, with its limited carrying capacity.

The Hackberry blacksmith and travelers that they met in the West also warned of the dangers, telling them to attempt only a night crossing, as the heat would surely be too great in the daytime. They originally planned to follow the advice they had received. However, their crude acetylene gas headlight failed part way across the desert and, since there was no moonlight, they "curled up among the cacti and went to sleep," Effie wrote in her journal.

It was customary to cross the desert in small groups to ensure the safety of all. Effie made arrangements with two autoists to join them, but when she and her mother arrived at the rendezvous location, their partners were nowhere to be found. Not to be deterred by this setback, they began their solo journey west through the barren landscape.

Effie frequently wrote about her tendency to get lost. Most often it was just inconvenient, but getting lost in the Mojave Desert had much more serious potential. And get lost in the desert she did. In 1915 this desert trail had no road signs, nor any other markings or monuments, to indicate the route. As the wind blew the desert sands around, trails became obscured or obliterated, and even seasoned travelers lost their way.

For the directionally impaired, crossing this great desert presented a special challenge. As Effie herself wryly noted:

"Anyone but I could have followed the correct route across the desert by the abandoned inner tube boxes. The hot sand was death to the 1915 vintage of patches, and they dropped off tubes like leaves in a wind storm. As usual I had to get lost and crossed the desert the hard way. We drank all the water from one sack after we got started the next morning and when

I reached for the other one something had rubbed a hole in it and it was drier than we were.

"It kept getting hotter and hotter and I kept getting loster and loster (to coin a word). It seemed to be at least 140 in the shade—if there was any to be found. Purely imaginary specks in the sky became buzzards joyfully hoping for the worst. My tongue was surely five times its normal size and I knew I had traveled hundreds of miles in a circle. I felt I should apologize to mother for leading her to this awful death and get her forgiveness before we passed through the pearly gates. Each bleached cow skull grinned at us in an evil way as if to say 'it won't be long now Effie, it's later than you think.' Ugh!

"We had not been traveling over two hours but it is surprising how many horrors can be compressed into that length of time. We saw more specks in the distance, more buzzards coming to the feast. There was nothing imaginary about these specks. They grew and grew until they turned into Mexican section hands, none of whom could speak English. They stood welcoming us with grins but then the wolf grinned at little Red Riding Hood and see what happened to her.

"I was frightened still and in spite of the temperature cold chills were playing tag up and down my spine. The largest and most ferocious looking Mexican came forward and I wondered if I should start shooting or give up our lives without a struggle. I did not shoot, probably a case of buck ague, a lucky break as our welcomer turned out to be a perfectly charming gentleman. He made me understand the water sack could be mended with a tire patch and then proceeded to do it for me. He then filled both sacks from a barrel of aqua pura although by then we were not at all particular about the pura part. He drew a map in the sand which even I could understand and sent us off in the right direction with his blessing. Viva La Mexico!"

Once out of the desert, California looked like the Promised Land to the weary women. The ride west to the coast was uneventful and a pleasure compared to what they had experienced before. Effie was ecstatic:

Proudly displaying their New York City banner, Effie pours Atlantic Ocean water into the Pacific on a Los Angeles beach. This ceremony was a custom practiced by most transcontinental travelers in the pre-World War I period. (Photo used by permission of the Hotchkiss Family Estate) I ♡ this!

"California, and something resembling good roads again, only good was not a strong enough adjective considering what we had been driving over. They were glorious, magnificent and I could hardly make up my mind which would give us the most enjoyment, drive slow and savor every inch or give the long suffering motorcycle its head and really allow it to shake a wheel."

The Hotchkisses made quick progress across southern California toward their next destination—Los Angeles and the Pacific Ocean. Upon reaching the sandy shores of the Pacific in early August, Effie followed the custom of pouring a bottle of Atlantic Ocean water she had carried for four thousand miles into the western sea. To ensure that they weren't taken for mere local riders out on a short jaunt, they proudly displayed their New York City banner across the front of the sidecar.

Effie and Avis took some time to tour the Los Angeles region, later telling a newspaper reporter that they fell in love with the area with its paved roads, mild weather, and many scenic wonders.

But they still had to go north along the rugged California coast nearly 400 miles to San Francisco. Although California roads were a significant improvement over what they had encountered in preceding weeks, they still faced many challenges.

Driving from Los Angeles to San Francisco was very much an adventure a century ago, and skilled drivers set forth on what was optimistically called the Pacific Highway to see how quickly they could navigate between the two cities. In August 1915 movie star and race car driver Anita King, known as "The Paramount Girl" and a darling of the press, set a record by making the drive between Los Angeles and San Francisco in 17 hours in her Kissell Kar. She then continued on her cross-country trip to New York, arriving 49 days later. The Los Angeles to San Francisco route was a favorite road for sanctioned endurance runs, a popular form of motorized competition a century ago.

OUR TRAVELERS didn't have to wait long before difficult conditions appeared again on their itinerary. Effie and Avis encountered the main obstacle shortly after they began their northward trek. San Marcos Pass, through the Santa Ynez Mountains, is an easy drive today on scenic route 154, but in the 1910s the road through these mountains was a dirt trail which challenged the best drivers.

Effie had two options: take a long detour around the mountains or attempt the trail over them, which was in poor shape due to construction. As she wrote:

> "This time we had a choice of two detours, leave it to California to do things in a big way. One detour would take us over the San Marcos Pass, which, we were told, was very beautiful, also dangerous, and could not be made on a motorcycle."

That last statement settled it; up and at 'em and over the San Marcos Pass they went.

"We met a man at the foot of the pass who told that the scenery was magnificent and we would never regret having chosen that route. He lied in his teeth, I regretted every mile of it although the motorcycle made it with less effort than many of the 1915 model cars. I had the gear ratio changed before leaving home and while it undoubtedly did slow the motorcycle down on level roads it was a marvelous help in hill climbing. Mother took a few peeks over the edge of the mountain and did not like what she saw, decided she would be safer afoot. She walked a good part of the way and so did many car passengers."

But make San Francisco they did. The motorcycle needed much repair, so they rented a room and left the bike at the local Harley-Davidson dealer. The women spent time touring the city and, naturally, attended the Panama-Pacific Exposition—one of their reasons for making the trip in the first place.

Organizers of the Panama-Pacific International Exposition and the City of San Francisco outdid themselves in every possible way to create this extravaganza. The exposition, which served as the 1915 World's Fair, was primarily meant to mark the opening of the Panama Canal, which had overnight made the Pacific coast an equal trading partner with the Atlantic. It's hard to fully appreciate today the difference the canal made to America's West Coast economy, as well as in the minds of westerners. No longer would they be playing second fiddle to New York or other eastern ports. Major cities up and down the West Coast could now think of themselves as world players.

The city also wanted to show that it had completely rebuilt itself after the devastating 1906 earthquake, so the exposition site was a large land-filled area on the waterfront in what is now the Marina District. They used an amazing 300,000 cubic yards of fill, much of it debris from the earthquake. Exhibitors from around the country were anxious to showcase the latest amazing discoveries and inventions.

As technically remarkable as the exposition was, it was even more of a visual treat with stunning lighting displays and architectural delights. The most spectacular was the Tower of Jewels. It was 43 stories tall and was covered with over a hundred thousand dangling colored glass "jewels". These reflected sunlight as the breezes moved them, and shone with the reflected light of spotlights directed at the exterior of the building at night, creating a stunning feast for the eyes.

Nothing was spared to make the entire experience unforgettable for the nearly 18 million attendees, the great majority of whom arrived by train. Nearly every American celebrity or leading citizen attended the fair—Theodore Roosevelt, Helen Keller, Thomas Edison, Al Jolson, Buffalo Bill Cody and dozens of other VIPs and celebrities.

The first transcontinental long distance phone line was completed to San Francisco in 1915, and one attraction of the fair was to speak live from there to someone in New York. Thomas Edison made the first transcontinental phone call at the start of the Exposition. I can easily imagine that Effie and her mother at least attempted to telephone their family back in the East, in addition to telegraphs and letters that they had most likely been faithfully sending home.

WITH THE MOTORCYCLE repaired, having tasted exotic foods across the city, and having "enjoyed every moment spent at the Fair right down to the blisters on our feet," the time came for the Hotchkisses to head back east. They had another very long and difficult trip ahead of them, and it was critical to arrive in New York City before cold weather set in.

The day before they departed, they decided to take one last look at Golden Gate Park. This decision changed Effie's life in a way that she couldn't have imagined. As she put it, she ran into, and partly over, her future. For, while she was taking this last ride through the park, a man stepped off the boardwalk into the motorcycle's path. Effie couldn't avoid running over his foot, but she was driving so slowly that he wasn't injured. She helped him pick himself up, dust himself off, and they introduced themselves.

The three of them enjoyed a relaxing dinner that evening to mark their last day in the big city. During dinner, Effie and the western cowboy boasted of the many charms and attractions of their respective parts of the country. Effie spoke on New York's behalf, the accident victim represented Oregon. After dinner, they exchanged pleasantries, said good bye and went their separate ways.

Early the next morning Effie and Avis packed their gear in and on their extensively repaired motorcycle and sidecar, took one last look around them to make their mental images of San Francisco permanent, put on their riding gear, and headed east. It was a very emotional moment. Both women had fallen in love with California and San Francisco. They were simultaneously excited and apprehensive about the more than 3,000 miles that lay ahead of them, with the adventures, difficulties, and dangers that they could now more realistically expect.

Avis and Effie followed the Lincoln Highway almost all the way back to New York State. Fortunately for them, the highway over the Altamont Pass just east of San Francisco had been completed earlier that year, allowing a simplified route east through California. They had fewer major transportation incidents on the return trip, although they did come across many interesting people and were involved in several memorable experiences.

Near Sparks, Nevada, they encountered a local woman rancher who was so enthralled by the idea of these two women traveling by motorcycle and sidecar, a contraption she had never seen before, that she insisted they stay with her for awhile. While there, Effie gave the woman a ride in the sidecar to the local town for supplies, and her passenger was thrilled. To a woman who had lived in the barren wilderness of Nevada, raising sheep and struggling to survive in the harsh desert conditions, this unexpected introduction to the 20th century must have, indeed, been a wonderful diversion from her normal routine.

Their hostess talked the Hotchkisses into staying a couple more days so that the neighbors could get together with them. One thing led to another, and the following morning Effie happily participated in a neighborhood rabbit hunt, especially since one of the neighbors was a "handsome young animal with a mane of curly black hair."

As they were walking through the desert, the young man, much to Effie's chagrin, suddenly pulled her back and told her not to move. When she began to protest, he pointed out a rattlesnake right in front of them that was coiled and ready to strike. He shot the snake, and Effie learned a valuable lesson that would come in handy in years to

Effie and Avis pause for a picture in front of the House of Hopper Harley-Davidson agency in Salt Lake City, while following the Lincoln Highway back to New York. Note that as late as 1915 motorcycle dealers also sold bicycles. (Photo used by permission of the Hotchkiss Family Estate)

come. After a feast of rabbit and sage grouse, they all went to Reno to enjoy the night life.

Avis and her daughter rode the Lincoln Highway to Salt Lake City, where they visited the House of Hopper Harley-Davidson dealer and had their picture taken. Effie doesn't mention any problems in the Great Basin, but the *Salt Lake Tribune* advised in September of 1915—the period when the women would have been traveling east through that region—that roads across Utah and Wyoming were "all muddy." Effie may have considered roads that were simply muddy to be the norm and not warranting worry or note.

EAST OF CHEYENNE, conditions got better. The Lincoln Highway across much of Nebraska had been described as being in better shape and less of a challenge to negotiate than in other states. It was flat and relatively smooth (except, of course, following a rain) and easy to follow. Across much of the state, the Platte River was on one side of the road, and Union Pacific railroad tracks were on the other. Telegraph poles, which now included the new transcontinental telephone wire, lined the highway, making it easy to follow, even for someone with a propensity for getting lost.

Their return trip across the high plains and prairies was uneventful, though certainly not easy in comparison to today's standards. But traveling during that period did have its benefits. The pair made it a point to stop and eat alongside the road as much as possible. I can easily imagine a typical lunch stop under the endless skies of the prairies. Complete silence surrounded them, broken only by the song of the meadowlark and the occasional warning whistles of prairie dogs when they spotted a hawk riding the thermal updrafts high overhead.

They would have heard only a few other human noises such as the occasional sound of a far away train whistle rolling for miles across the open countryside. Nights spent camping in the solitude of 1910s rural America would also have been marvelous. The yipping coyotes and the hooting owls, along with millions of insects, created a symphony unlike anything they would hear in an auditorium.

Riding through the fertile landscape at the peak of the annual growth cycle, the Plains were a delightful place to be. Bobolinks and bluebirds would have flown along with the riders from one wooden

Avis, with a look of resigned frustration, after becoming stuck yet once again in deep mud. It was up to Effie to free the heavy machine and sidecar from the mire. (Photo used by permission of the Hotchkiss Family Estate)

fence post to the next, following Effie and Avis as they motored peacefully through the countryside.

Just west of Kearney, Nebraska, they crossed the halfway point between San Francisco and Boston. A sign indicating that it was 1,733 miles west to San Francisco and an equal distance east to Boston was installed soon after they passed through. Kearney capitalized on its unique location, and the Halfway City eventually became a tourist stop based on its position on the Lincoln Highway.

In eastern Nebraska, the corn was as high as the proverbial elephant's eye. Though the year continued to be wet, the crops survived and even prospered in the hot and humid Great Plains summer. They had smooth sailing until Iowa, where they once again encountered mud, flooding, and washed out bridges.

Effie was by no means the only 1915 cross-country traveler to encounter, and later write about, the terrible condition of Iowa's roads. Emily Post and others also mentioned the tendency of the Hawkeye State's roads to turn into a deep gumbo mud immediately following a rain.

In a September 1915 editorial the Iowa City *Daily Press* took great offense at Post's comments, suggesting that she come back at a time when there hadn't been so much rain and stating that she would then find the roads more to her liking. But of course the point of her criticism was the need to have roads that didn't turn into a swampy quagmire every time it rained.

Another Iowa newspaper was more willing to admit that the state had problems with its roads. The Council Bluffs *Daily Nonpareil* noted that one-half of all Indiana's road mileage was gravel. In 1915 Iowa, as it pointed out, only one out of every175 miles was improved in some manner. The remaining roads were unimproved dirt surfaces.

Perhaps Effie and Avis read Post's magazine articles upon returning in the fall of 1915 from their own trip on some of the same roads. They may have felt some kindred spirit, though not too much. After all, Miss Post took her trip in a fancy European road car with her son as chauffeur and mechanic, spending nights in the best hotels and eating meals prepared in the better restaurants they encountered. On the other hand, Effie and Avis had made the trip in a much more spartan style.

EFFIE DESCRIBED A frustrating incident involving "a bridge that wasn't there" on one of Iowa's infamous dirt roads:

> "They were working on it and had the road torn up for about three miles in either direction from the bridge. There was a detour around the bridge-to-be. I had been keeping track of the detours but gave up at around the seven hundredth. This one was a honey, sort of a switchback affair. At the bottom of the first down-you-go the side car parted company with the motorcycle. I looked the debris over, got the side car out of the way, stuck the broken connection in my pocket and headed east while mother retired to a dry spot under a tree and got out the inevitable tatting.
>
> "The mud was thick and the road looked to have been stirred with a big spoon and then left to its fate, the stirring having brought up a lot of assorted rocks from the depths. I had not gone very far when the motorcycle and I took a header. This was quite humiliating as I had no inferiority complex when it came to my ability to handle a motorcycle. I was not hurt, who could be landing in the soft goo, but I cried from pure rage. I

got on again and the road got worse, if that was possible, and I had another spill."

Effie slipped and slid for miles in these conditions, her rear wheel throwing up a rooster tail of mud while plowing a six-inch rut through the muck. Eventually, she made it to a blacksmith's shop, only to find that he could not perform the necessary repair. She had to retrace her tortuous route to inform her mother that she was going to ride west as far as necessary to find somebody who could mend the broken part. After much trouble, Effie did locate a craftsman who could repair the broken rods.

But that was only half of the problem. She then had to use what little strength she had left to wrestle the machine through the mud back to her mother and the broken sidecar and lie in the mud to reconnect the various parts. Try to imagine the ordeal of working in the muck, tormented by mosquitoes and every biting and crawling creature known to exist in Iowa, while trying to make repairs that would have been a challenge in a clean well-equipped repair shop. Effie's unconquerable spirit shined its brightest that day!

She made the repairs and they once again rode east on the Lincoln. By 1915 Harley-Davidson dealers, or agents, as they were called then, formed an extensive network. The E. H. Hall Agency in Cedar Rapids, Iowa, might have been a welcome stop to make repairs necessary for the long trip that still lay ahead of them. The muddy conditions followed them all the way to Chicago, where Effie needed a truck to extricate them from the mire. The fact that it was a truck and not a team of horses that came to their rescue was evidence that they were east of the Mississippi.

RIDING ACROSS THE country as they did, Effie and Avis saw the world, not as it might have been portrayed in books or magazines, but how it really looked, felt, and smelled in person. They suffered in the heat, sloshed through the mud, and saw the struggles of working class Americans scratching a living from the reluctant earth. They interacted with and saw farmers, blacksmiths, garage owners, and small businessmen of every type working hard to survive and provide for their families.

One of the more poignant scenes Effie describes occurred while riding through coal mining country.

> "The most depressing scene we encountered was a coal mining town we passed through in the rain. Whenever I hear the coal miners being cussed for going on strike I think of that town. Maybe things have improved for the miners since then and I sincerely hope so. In the rain, that town was horrible and I doubt sunshine would have made much improvement.
>
> "The shacks were built in long rows and were indescribably decrepit and flimsy, not one had a distinguishing mark of any kind, the rain mixed with coal dust dripped off each one in the same dreary way. Not a blade of green anywhere, just coal dust. The children scampered at our approach like little wild animals but lacked a wild animal's cleanliness. Not their fault, poor little tots, wild animals had cleaner surroundings.
>
> "The few women I saw looked bedraggled and dispirited and I could not blame them. I was nearly in the same state just passing through this nightmare of a town. The rain made black spatters in the road and gloom covered everything with a dirty blanket."

Upon reaching Ohio, the women left the Lincoln Highway and retraced their route through Cleveland and Buffalo. They took time to visit Niagara Falls before heading east across New York. On October 11 they once again stopped at Ossining, New York, where Effie's brother Everett had ridden his motorcycle north from the city to meet them. They recorded the emotional occasion with a photograph in a symbolic closing of the circle. The next day found them in Brooklyn, greeted by the tears and laughter of family and friends.

THE HOTCHKISSES arrived back home on a crisp October day with autumn in its full glory. Having left New York in early May, their trip took them from the moist, green freshness of Spring to the cold rains of Fall, with falling colorful leaves honoring them upon their return like confetti dropped from the heights for returning heroes.

After negotiating 9,000 miles of some of the worst roads and weather imaginable over a period of five months, returning was a bittersweet affair for Effie. Avis was undoubtedly happy to be home again, but she had also undergone a metamorphosis because of the trip. Neither would ever be the same. Having established the record as the first people to make a round-trip journey across the continent on a motorcycle and sidecar, they had a sense of pride in an accomplishment that they achieved only with great effort.

Probably unbeknownst to Avis and Effie at the time, another parent/child duo was making a round-trip motorcycle and sidecar journey across the continent during the Summer and Fall of 1915, beginning and ending their trip just weeks after the Hotchkisses. William and Walter Kellogg, who also lived near New York City, made a nearly 11,000 mile circle of America with Walter operating the machine and his father William accompanying him in the sidecar. As reported in the *Orange County* (New York) *Times-Press*, they departed New York on June 11 and returned on November 22, 1915. The Kelloggs maintained a detailed log of their journey. In it they noted that they rode 10,912 miles, used 305 gallons of gasoline, 135 quarts of oil, and were actually under way for 39 days, for a very impressive daily average of 280 miles.

ONCE HOME, Effie set about sharing her story with the public through an article that the *New York Sun* requested after learning of the successful trip. In it she stressed the positive and did not dwell on the dangerous and difficult situations they had faced. She clearly intended to tell a story that highlighted the enjoyable and interesting, leaving out the darker side.

But she faced a difficult transition coming back to New York City after experiencing the open spaces and attitudes of the West. Prior to the trip, Effie had ridden the subway daily to get to work, but now she could barely stand the crowds and confined areas. Her job had lost whatever allure it had had, and it was only with much resolve and discipline that she managed to go to work every day in the confining towers of Wall Street.

Effie's office may as well have been a dungeon; she made the daily trip to sit at a desk for eight hours with little joy and enthusiasm.

Effie and Avis complete the circle. Photo taken in Ossining, New York where they departed from family and friends five months earlier. Photo by Everett Hotchkiss. Visible on the sidewalk next to the motorcycle is a gasoline dispensing device. (Photo used by permission of the Hotchkiss Family Estate)

She longed for the West, with its vistas and lack of crowds. Effie wanted to smell sage brush and pine forests, not the polluted air of a large city. She longed for the music of coyotes under a starlit sky and the symphonic splendor of songbirds such as they had heard on cool prairie mornings.

THE DOOR INTO another life unexpectedly opened a crack one day when she received a letter with an Oregon postmark. Her mother and sister waited impatiently for her to return from work so that she could open the envelope to see who it was from. As it turned out, the letter was from the man Effie had bumped into with her motorcycle on the San Francisco beach.

The article she wrote for the *New York Sun* had been printed by other newspapers, including one seen by the Oregon rancher, cattleman, and charming widower, Mr. Guy Johnston. The article noted Effie's home address, so Johnston sent a note to her telling how much he had enjoyed dinner with her and Avis in San Francisco. He also reminded Effie that, if she ever made it to the West again, she should be sure to come to Oregon to see for herself all the wonderful things he had described during their brief time together in San Francisco.

Effie didn't receive the letter with complete elation. She was a bit put out by what seemed like Johnston's excessive bragging, so she felt the need to respond with some boasts of her own about New York. In her first letter, she penned a long list of virtues of both states, giving New York the clear winning edge.

The long distance communication continued for some months, until finally Effie challenged Mr. Johnston to come to New York saying she would personally show him all that he was missing. All this at a time when she was no longer convinced that the big city was all it was cracked up to be; she dreamed constantly of the opportunity to get back to the West somehow.

JOHNSTON ACCEPTED the invitation and sent her a telegram, saying that he would be in New York on the day before Thanksgiving of 1916 and asking her to meet him at Grand Central Station. At first, Effie questioned her sanity in having answered his very first letter and having carried on the long distance relationship for so long. Now it was different; he was actually in New York and Effie pondered what she should do.

She showed him the town and all the marvelous New York entertainment that just couldn't be found in the frontier wilds of eastern Oregon, and Mr. Johnston had a great time. They had a whirlwind courtship, and, in nearly no time, Johnston asked her to marry him. In fact, over a two week period he pestered her so much, and her friends were so enthusiastic about this western cowboy, that she agreed.

Guy unknowingly sealed the deal one day just before Christmas when he brought Effie a special gift. She describes it this way:

> "One day when he came to the office to meet me for lunch, after a busy morning of sightseeing with mother, he handed me a leather case containing a beautiful shot gun and it still remains my most cherished possession. Any man who had sense enough to buy me a shot gun instead of some frilly feminine thing was my kind of man and I wanted him for keeps. Would you call this another version of a shotgun wedding?"

Effie was ready to embrace her future. She knew that New York City and the experience she had known there represented the past, and she was anxious to move on to the next phase of her life. She also fully understood that her future lay in the American West, not as a clerk on Wall Street.

Effie and Guy married a few days later, and he returned to Oregon to be with his three nearly-grown children for Christmas. To finalize all necessary arrangements at work and home, Effie stayed in New York for four months before finally heading west once again. She settled one final issue prior to leaving, and this involved her traveling companion and friend—her mother Avis. With brother Everett running their father's farm in the Catskills and sister Avis moved away, Effie and her mother decided that she should go west with Effie to live on the Oregon ranch.

WITH CONSIDERABLE emotional difficulty, Effie sold the beloved motorcycle that had so faithfully carried them on their adventure. But she knew that, at least in the short term, motorcycles were also a part of her past.

They took the train to Parma, Idaho, just across the border from Oregon and a ranch owned by Guy's parents, where they spent some time before moving to their own place. The train deposited them at the depot in the dark, and when Effie saw the muddy streets and the tacky false-fronted buildings in daylight, she was not at all certain she had made a wise choice in moving to Oregon sight-unseen.

Effie Hotchkiss Johnston and her mother Avis many years later at their Oregon ranch. (Photo used by permission of the Hotchkiss Family Estate)

Guy's extended family was larger than anything Effie was used to, and the first few months in Oregon were a whirlwind, with a houseful of gregarious in-laws keeping life filled to the brim. In 1920 they lived in Malheur County in the state's sparsely populated southeast corner. They relocated as opportunities arose and, by 1930, Guy and Effie had moved to Klamath County in south central Oregon.

Over the years, their ranch life ranged from raising beef cattle to growing potatoes; whatever it took to make a living. In the pre-World War II period, rural Oregon was a largely undeveloped region with poor roads and where many people had no electricity or indoor plumbing. Effie worked hard as a rancher's wife and a mother, but she loved every minute of it and would not have changed a thing.

SHE LIVED A FULL and happy life in Oregon, complete with many adventures and hardships. One of the first opportunities to prove her skills as a farmer came very soon after she arrived. Guy had to leave to pick up his youngest child from a boarding school and suggested that he would have a neighbor come over to milk the cows in his absence. Effie was annoyed at the obvious implication that she couldn't handle this chore herself. She convinced Guy that she knew all about milking cows, and he reluctantly agreed to leave it in her hands.

Effie later wrote about her first experience as a dairy farmer.

"With a shining milk pail in my hand I started for the cow shed. The cows looked surprised to see me. Before I was through with them they were too worn out to show any emotion. Carefully balancing myself on a one legged contraption I set down on the wrong side of the cow. How was I to know cows had right and wrong sides? And one legged stools! Wood must have been awfully scarce when they were built but surely it would not have taken very much to make them with three legs.

"Balancing a one legged stool is an art that has to be learned. One to get ready, two to get set and three to go and I went. I pulled, the cow kicked and the stool collapsed. After this process had been repeated several times I decided to try the other side of Bossy, maybe the floor was a little softer over there. This turned out to be the move the cow had been suggesting all the time. I was two hours doing the milking and had milk in my boots, down the back of my neck, and in my hair, but I left the cows dry and bewildered."

Effie never owned or rode a motorcycle again after leaving New York City. Her life had changed in every possible way with her move to Oregon. With the financial struggles of being a small rancher, raising a family, and uncertainties such as wars and the Depression, there was little time or money for anything that didn't help farm the land and bring in food and cash.

They needed to earn money however they could when prices for milk, hay, potatoes, beef, timber, and the various other products they labored to produce fell due to market conditions, so Guy was often away at odd jobs. Effie stayed behind to run the ranch and their other businesses. Ironically, one of the more financially rewarding jobs Guy got was a contract from the state to help construct roads in eastern Oregon.

Effie Hotchkiss was like many people through the ages who were on the leading edge of movement into frontier areas. She loved the wild and free natural landscape that surrounded her in Oregon, an extension of her own unfettered and expansive personality. She made many references to activities that she enjoyed very much, such as camping, trout fishing, hunting, picking wild berries (and encountering the occasional bear), and exploring the countryside on the back roads.

She and her family lived the life they wanted, one that allowed the unstructured and unregulated freedom to do what they wished to a large degree, knowing full well that the consequences—good or ill— would be totally their own responsibility. The work was back-breaking, but the rewards of close family and good friends were many. Effie would not have had it any other way.

In her journal, she frequently noted the western lifestyle and western attitudes. She turned into a proud Westerner, and her writings betrayed no nostalgia for New York City and her old life. A century ago, the West was still being populated by people like her who had moved from the East looking for a place where they could build new lives. Those who stayed abandoned their eastern ways and adopted the ways of a Westerner. She quoted two poems about the West in her writings; this one seems to perfectly reflect her outlook after decades of hard work on the ranch.

> Out where the sun beats down a little stronger,
> Out where they work about four hours longer,
> Out where they raise the corn and clover,
> But have nothing to show when the year is over,
> That's where the West begins.
> Out where the mavericks bellow and bawl,
> And the farmer weeps at the long freight haul,
> For he knows that the railroad will get it all,
> That's where the West begins.
> Out where the farmers rave and cuss,
> But do not strike and raise a fuss,
> As they pay for goods sold Pittsburg plus,
> Where things are in a gosh awful muss,
> That's where the West begins.[2]

Effie's brother Everett and his family also moved to Oregon a few years later, and they were a welcome addition to the large circle

---

[2] By J.C. Erlander

of family and friends. Guy and Effie had one daughter, Jean, born in a tent in the Oregon wilderness in 1918 while Guy was away on a road building job. Avis lived to her mid-nineties, and was a welcome and constant presence at the several Oregon ranches that Effie and Guy operated.

A misdiagnosis by an Oregon doctor many years later was instrumental in the world's knowing more of Effie's story. The physician erroneously told her that her heart was failing and that she had just months to live. He advised her to use this remaining time to relax and perhaps write the story of her life. To an active woman and mother helping to run an Oregon ranch, this prescription was the worst possible medicine to swallow. She would much rather have been on a tractor or behind a team of horses than at a desk staring at a typewriter keyboard. But eventually the words began to flow, and we are fortunate indeed to have her account of the motorcycle expedition and her marvelous life story, written with just the sort of wit and humorous irreverence that were so much a part of who she was.

Thus, virtually all the information about Effie and her very interesting life comes from her, not secondhand sources. Despite the passage of so many years, her memory was clear and the information she provided in her journal is more than adequate to fully appreciate what she and her mother experienced and the difficulties they encountered and overcame. Beyond the details it provides, her journal documents what a wonderfully positive, witty, and resourceful person she was. By the way, in true Effie Hotchkiss style, she lived many more years after the doctor predicted her imminent demise.

It is interesting to look back at Effie's adventure and her response to the challenges she faced in comparing her writings. In her journal, she went into much more detail describing those incidents that posed great difficulty and even danger. She wrote about them in her usual upbeat manner, but her later journal fortunately provides us with a more inclusive account of her trip—the good and the bad.

Guy died in 1946 of cancer, at the age of 73. Effie was remarried ten years later to Earl Terpening, whom she also outlived.

She lived an active life in her senior years, including taking a lengthy boat trip to Alaska. Most notably, Effie became very involved in volunteer activities. She was a regular at the Roseburg Veterans Administration Hospital in southwestern Oregon, helping wounded vets.

On a sad day in 1967, on her way home from the hospital where she had just donated several hours helping patients, she collapsed and died at the age of 78. The journey of a marvelous woman who lived life to the fullest, and who was, in turn, admired and loved by everyone who met her, had come to an end.

IN 2002, EFFIE and Avis were publicly recognized and honored by a new generation of admirers in the unlikely setting of Buckhannon, West Virginia, eighty-seven years after their trip. The American Motorcyclist Association was holding its third annual Women & Motorcycling conference there. The symposium that year covered many issues relative to female riders, and, very appropriately, was dedicated to these two outstanding adventurous travelers and pioneering women.

Many female motorcycle enthusiasts today are proud to use Effie as an example of the enduring spirit and can-do attitude required if one is to chase her dreams successfully. What really makes her such a special person is that she faced life head on, an outstanding quality no matter the situation or the dream chased.

Mule trains such as this one photographed in Nevada in 1915 were still common sights in the barren American Southwest less than a century ago (Photo used with permission of the University of Michigan Bentley Library)

A lonely worker paints identifying symbols on telegraph poles along the Lincoln Highway in the vast open spaces of Wyoming. (Photo used with permission of University of Michigan Bentley Library)

The Van Buren Sisters:
Out to Change America

—◦◦◦—

Johnnie get your gun, get your gun, get your gun,
Take it on the run, on the run, on the run;
Hear them calling you and me;
Every son of liberty.
Over there, over there,
Send the word, send the word over there -
That the Yanks are coming,
The Yanks are coming,
The drums rum-tumming
Everywhere.
So prepare, say a prayer,
Send the word, send the word to beware.
We'll be over, we're coming over,
And we won't come back till it's over
Over there.[1]

I didn't think there were this many people in all of Springfield!"
Augusta Van Buren grumbled as she wiped the dripping sweat from
her brow with the back of her muddy glove. A curiosity-filled crowd
had gathered to watch her fix the chain on her motorcycle in the late
evening drizzle. However, after having ridden for eight hours in the

---

[1] George M. Cohan and Leo Feist, 1917.

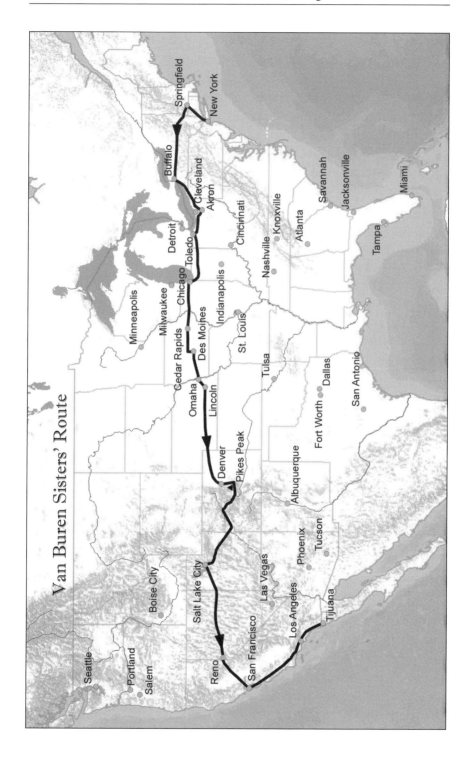

Van Buren Sisters' Route

rain and mud from New York City to Springfield, Massachusetts, she was in no mood to be the center of attention.

It was an inconvenient time for the drive chain to break, but it was the sort of repair that she and her sister Adeline had performed countless times in the past. However, no matter how routine such repairs were to these adventurous siblings, seeing a woman repair a motorcycle was unusual and quite remarkable to most Americans. The sisters had just completed the first day of a grand journey across the country, but, while they motored toward San Francisco astride their Indians with no misgivings, the rest of the country followed with great interest and some concern.

Augusta and Adeline Van Buren, or Gussie and Addie as their family and close friends called them, were born into a solid middle-class family in New York City. The sisters told a reporter from the *Chicago Tribune* that they were distant descendants of the country's eighth President, Martin Van Buren, who served from 1837–1841. Van Buren was the first President born under the flag of the United States of America instead of a British colony. He served in many official capacities in all levels of government, including as Vice President under Andrew Jackson.

I can imagine that the women rode their motorcycles north on the Post Road to Kinderhook, New York, to visit Lindenwald, Van Buren's beloved farm, and his nearby gravesite. Despite this distant connection with the former President, the sisters had to make it on their own merits, not with inherited wealth or fame.

Early in their lives, the sisters broke out of the mold in which many middle- or upper middle-class urban girls found themselves. While they most likely partook in music lessons and learned the prescribed skills and behaviors expected of well-rounded young ladies, they opened doors that some other girls found closed.

Their father, Frank Van Buren, made sure that, in addition to mastering parlor skills, they also were exposed to a wide variety of physical and athletic activities. Participating in them helped develop the abilities and confidence they would need in the world beyond the cultured and insulated society of the late Victorian Era. They learned to box at age seven and became adept at canoeing, riding horses, swimming and diving, ice skating, and various other endeavors. They worked hard,

Lindenwald, President Martin Van Buren's home located near Kinderhook, New York. It is protected in the Martin Van Buren National Historic Site. (Photo by author)

competed in several of these sports and were proud of the prizes and medals they won. The sisters quickly adapted to physically demanding outdoor challenges.

In 1913 they took up motorcycling with a passion. In a 1916 newspaper interview, Adeline voiced the opinion that riding motorcycles was a natural progression from their earlier participation in outdoor activities. Ever the enthusiastic motorcyclist, she confessed that riding "has supplanted all other sports and now reigns supreme as it has for three years."

Both sisters were accomplished motorcyclists who were able to handle their machines as well as any rider. They had ridden extensively on congested urban streets, dodging the thousands of cars and horses that turned New York City's thoroughfares into a dangerous hodgepodge of traffic. They had also motored on deserted back roads where mud and ruts were the norm.

In the 1910s mechanical problems were all too common, but these young women were able to repair their machines as necessary. They had no qualms about riding long distances at a time when the nearest help might mean a long walk should problems arise.

It was with the broad and adventurous perspective learned in their youth that the Van Buren sisters participated in the world around them. By the summer of 1916 Augusta and Adeline had settled into successful adult, professional lives. Augusta, 32 years of age, worked in a business office and 26-year old Adeline was an English teacher in a New York City elementary school.

As they matured, the women also developed a spirit of public service and pride in their country. Foreseeing America's involvement in World War I, they were active in civic organizations such as the Special Relief Society, organized in 1915 to enlist American women for national preparedness duties, and the National Security League, another organization involved in what became known as the "Preparedness Movement."

WITH MOTORCYCLING having evolved into such a passion for the sisters, and their desire to test themselves in the realm of physical activities, one can easily understand their desire to make a transcontinental motorcycle trip. They had been riding extensively for three years, and, in fact, had covered close to 9,000 miles in 1915 alone. They were ready for a new challenge.

Anyone who shares a similar yearning for adventure can understand their desire to expand their horizons beyond the roads of New York and New England. They certainly wanted to cross the country on their Indians for the adventure, excitement, challenges, and lifelong treasury of memories and stories that would result from such an undertaking. But the Van Buren sisters had two additional reasons to make the trip. They wanted to awaken a nation that they felt was in denial about the imminent likelihood of war, and they wanted to prove to the U.S. Army that women could play an important role in the event of war.

The National Defense Act, which Congress passed in June 1916 authorizing an increase in the Army's troop level, partially satisfied members of the Preparedness Movement. But many activists felt that an increase in military strength was only part of the issue. Americans still needed to get ready for a possible war, and the Van Buren sisters would attempt to do their part in this educational effort by distributing Movement flyers to people they met along their cross country route.

They also had something more personal to prove. Augusta and Adeline felt that they and other women motorcyclists were fully qualified to perform courier duties as dispatch riders. They hoped that, by making an unassisted trip across the continent, they could convince the Army that they possessed these qualifications and that the Army would allow women to enlist for this duty.

As Adeline explained in a newspaper interview in Springfield:

"English women are doing motorcycle dispatch service in the battlefields of France, and we are trying to show American women that they can also help out in the same department, thereby making it possible for a greater number of men to be on the firing line."

The sisters were fully confident of their abilities and they resented being fenced in or restricted simply because they were female. They wanted to actively contribute in any future war, and through their trip they intended to prove their capabilities for such service.

Many women's groups and individuals were fighting for recognition of women's rights and a role for women in the military during this period, and the National Defense Act helped spotlight those very issues. One provision of the act was establishment of the Council of National Defense, comprised of the secretaries of War, Navy, Interior, Agriculture, Commerce, and Labor; all of whom were men.

In 1917, immediately after America entered the war, the Council's director created a Committee on Women's Defense Work. The subcommittee's stated purpose was: "To consider and advise how the assistance of the women of America may be made available in the prosecution of the war."

Doctor Anna Howard Shaw was 70 years old, with a long and distinguished vocation in women's suffrage activities (she was then the honorary president of the National American Woman Suffrage Association), became chairperson of the committee. The council also appointed nine members, most of whom were prominent suffragists. Two were from the anti-suffrage segment of American society—

Women's Suffrage

NOT ALL WOMEN supported the extension of voting rights to the female half of the population, and very many women did not support the idea of serving in the military. Some felt quite strongly that women's involvement in affairs outside of home and family would only serve to harm the family and threaten orderly society. In Logansport, Indiana, a farm wife left her husband for four months in 1916 because he strongly supported suffrage and she was a stalwart opponent. After the cooling off period, she returned home, and her husband observed, "The woman suffrage question will not be mentioned again in this household."

---

appointed, it seems obvious, to ensure that both sides were represented—and one was an outspoken pacifist.

That the Washington military establishment would appoint such a committee during a war speaks volumes about the impact women were having on influencing public debate on wide-ranging issues. Activists such as Susan B. Anthony, Elizabeth Cady Stanton, Anna Howard Shaw, Rachel Foster-Avery, Carrie Chapman Catt, and Alice Paul were in fact being heard, although change was coming more slowly than they had hoped. It is also very conceivable that Adeline and Augusta's untiring and outspoken efforts on behalf of women serving in the military helped pave the way for this council.

But conciliatory actions went only so far. When Ruth Law, a well-known pilot who held records for speed and endurance, tried to join the Army in 1917, she was flatly rejected. Then Secretary of War Newton Baker reportedly said of Miss Law's request, "We don't want women in the army."

Right up to the outbreak of World War I, suffragists and feminists in many nations pledged themselves to peace in an international gesture of women's solidarity. Shortly after the war began, the great majority of these women's rights groups declared support for their respective governments.

Many suffrage leaders organized women to further the war effort. They hoped that their demonstrated loyalty and work during the war would help ensure enactment of women's suffrage laws upon cessation of the hostilities. After all, one constant argument against women's right to vote was that females didn't carry the same burden of military service and national defense as men. Therefore, they didn't deserve the same level of involvement in voting or in governmental affairs. Many women's rights organizations saw the war as the way out of this dilemma.

MILITARY ESTABLISHMENTS around the world were in the transition stage of replacing horses with motorcycles as the preferred mount for dispatch riders. In Europe, the warring nations had already made the switch, and motorcycle dispatch riders were playing a critical role in the Signal Corps, carrying messages between line units and between field and headquarters staff. It was dangerous and demanding work, requiring courage, resourcefulness, dedication and, of course, great skill at riding motorcycles through appalling conditions, often under enemy fire.

Being assigned as a dispatch rider during the First World War was something to be taken very seriously. Although most Americans thought they knew about battlefield conditions, it would have been impossible to fully comprehend the carnage that was occurring at an unprecedented level unless one was actually on the front. Few Americans had been on the battlegrounds of France, Belgium, and Russia. Newspaper and magazine articles couldn't convey the brutal, visceral realities, and only those who had been there fully understood stories and poems written by veterans – such as "In Flanders Fields" by Canadian military Doctor John McCrae.

Captain William Henry Lowe Watson, a veteran who served as a dispatch rider for the British Army for seven months during the first year of combat, portrayed the dangers and discomforts in his 1915 book, *Adventures of a Despatch Rider* (as they were called in Britain). Perhaps the Van Buren sisters had read it and, despite its graphic depictions of battlefield conditions, still wanted to serve in that capacity.

Capt. Watson vividly described riding in the dark, on muddy roads, often under fire from snipers or artillery. He wrote of incidents in which confusion reigned, of a lack of accurate maps, and of mechanical breakdowns in hazardous situations. He described riding in unknown regions looking for units that had moved from their prior locations, and, of course, being in the bulls-eye for enemy combatants because he possessed battlefield operational knowledge and carried secret orders.

It was not a job for the weak-hearted or those unable to handle the considerable physical stresses. Capt. Watson provided many examples of the dispatch rider's duties and expectations. Getting a message from one unit to another was much easier said than done. A rider had to survive ambushes, shelling, impassable roads, unfamiliar country, language barriers, sentries who were trigger-happy and nervous, rain and snow, and darkness.

After serving in this capacity for seven months, including a northern European winter, on a motorcycle, Watson received a well-earned promotion and was assigned new duties. He described in some detail the qualities needed in motorcyclists serving on and near the front in several passages.

> "A clever despatch rider...knows exactly at which corner he is likely to be sniped, and hurries accordingly. He remembers, to a yard, where the sentries are."
>
> If the road is under shell fire, he recalls where the shells usually fall, the interval between the shells and the times of shelling. For there is order in everything, and particularly in German gunnery. Lastly, he does not race along with nose on handlebar. That is a trick practised only by despatch riders who are rarely under fire, who have come to a strange and alarming country from Corps or Army Headquarters. The experienced motor-cyclist sits up and takes notice the whole time. He is able at the end of his ride to give an account of all that he has seen on the way."

Watson not only presented an assessment of how a rider should conduct himself on the front, he also portrayed some of the dangerous realities in an understated, matter-of-fact manner.

> "Now, as I have told you, on a motor-cycle, if you are going rapidly, you cannot hear bullets or shells coming or even shells bursting unless they are very near. Running slowly

on top, with the engine barely turning over, you can hear everything. So I went slow and listened. Through the air came the sharp "woop-ving" of shrapnel bursting towards you, the most devilish sound of all. Some prefer the shriek of shrapnel to the dolorous wail and deep thunderous crash of high explosive. But nothing frightens me so much as the shrapnel-shriek."

Captain Watson's experiences gave him clear impressions as to the British motorcycle brands that were able to perform to the demands of dispatch riding. Some clearly fell short in these necessary qualities, but one company, in his opinion, produced a machine—the Blackburne—that fulfilled the mission in splendid fashion.

Watson also wrote about the competition that remained between the tried-and-tested use of horses for courier duty and the relatively short experience with motorcycles. Even in 1915 motorized vehicles sometimes just could not do what a rider on a horse could accomplish—much to the chagrin of motorcycle dispatch riders.

"It was at La Bassée that we had our first experience of utterly unrideable roads. North of the canal the roads were fair macadam in dry weather and to the south the main road Béthune-Beuvry-Annequin was of the finest pavé. Then it rained hard. First the roads became greasy beyond belief. Starting was perilous, and the slightest injudicious swerve meant a bad skid. Between Gorre and Festubert the road was vile.

"It went on raining, and the roads were thickly covered with glutinous mud. The front mud-guard of George's Douglas choked up with a lamentable frequency. The Blackburne alone, the finest of all motor-cycles, ran with unswerving regularity. Finally, to our heartburning sorrow, there were nights on which motor-cycling became impossible, and we stayed restlessly at home while men on the despised horse carried our despatches. This we could not allow for long."

British officers and dispatch riders came from the upper class and, though courier duty was dangerous and difficult, it did have its benefits. Captain Watson frankly admitted, in his own words, that they were a privileged lot in many ways:

> "More than a dozen Varsity men were thrown like Daniels into a den of mercenaries. We were awkwardly privileged persons—full corporals within a few days' service.
> "Motor-cycling gave superlative opportunities of freedom. Our duties were "flashy", and brought us into familiar contact with officers of rank. We were highly paid, and thought to have much money of our own. In short, we who were soldiers of no standing possessed the privileges that a professional soldier could win only after many years' hard work".

An October 2, 1914, *New York Times* article with a Paris dateline was filled with praise for the British riders. It read in part:

> "The generals in command of the Allies are full of praise for the dispatch riders, who, since the beginning of the battle of the Aisne, have kept up communications between the corps along the line. The dispatch riders are mostly volunteers from British universities, many of them wealthy youths who night and day have made dashes through a country infested with German cavalry, carrying messages."

The *New York Times* published at least six lengthy articles about British dispatch riders in late 1914 and 1915. Two articles in November 1914 were in the *Times'* widely read Sunday edition. Four articles were reprints of articles printed by *The Motor Cycle of London* magazine. One story spoke mostly of the terrible road conditions and dangers inherent in riding muddy roads, replete with artillery holes, in the dark, all the while dodging mounted cavalry units and truck convoys traveling on the same narrow lanes.

Other articles described the dangers inherent in the job, but clearly gave the duty a patina of excitement and even glamour. With bold headlines such as "Motor Cyclists Have Many Thrills in War" and "No Speed Limits For War Cyclists," the pieces were clearly meant to entertain and recruit as much as to present factual details.

For two years prior to Addie and Gussie's cross-country journey, newspapers covered the European War without pause, and many stories at least touched on dispatch riders. This probably made a strong impression on patriotic young Americans who loved the idea of great adventure combined with motorcycling.

One can reasonably assume that the Van Buren sisters read those articles. All of this coverage in their home town newspaper would not have escaped their attention. Reading the Sunday *New York Times* in particular was most likely a tradition in the Van Buren household as it was for many New Yorkers, and they would surely have noticed any headline about motorcycling or dispatch duties.

What is less clear is whether they would have seen a news report, making the rounds in April 1915, about a woman dispatch rider from Ireland. The Sunday *Milwaukee Journal* printed a large picture of a woman on a BSA motorcycle, with the headline: "Woman Dispatch Rider Who Fearlessly Carries Messages to Ulster Soldiers." The caption read:

> "Ulster's famous dispatch riders have a woman recruit. Miss P. Kingsborough, the first woman to volunteer her services to Ulster's cause, is carrying war dispatches the same as men. Miss Kingsborough is an expert cyclist and she carries her messages a-wheel."

If the siblings had seen this picture, they would have been absolutely confident that they also could perform the duties of dispatch rider, and perhaps this story, printed early in the course of the war, helped spark their desire.

They were, almost certainly, at least generally aware of the realities of being a motorcycle messenger. It is unlikely that they had any illusions about the task, nor a shortage of appreciation for the very real dangers and difficulties inherent in such assignments, though it is impossible to accurately imagine wartime dangers and conditions from the comforts of one's home.

The Van Buren sisters had ridden thousands of miles in the preceding three years, through all manner of bad roads and bad weather. They naturally did this without the interference of snipers and incoming artillery, but no new military enlistee has had combat experience; lack of battlefield expertise or experience has never disqualified wartime volunteers.

The sisters were intelligent, physically fit, courageous, excellent motorcyclists, mechanically skilled, undeterred by hardship and discomforts, possessed the ability to assess situations and respond accordingly, were patriotic, and they were ready and willing to serve. They clearly met every qualification except one: they were not males.

What must have been especially maddening is that the U.S. military eventually began recruiting experienced motorcyclists for courier duties. In January 1917 the Army sent notices to motorcycle clubs across the nation, urging them to receive training in the use of motorcycles to fill the possible need for dispatch riders should the nation go to war.

According to *Motor Cycle Illustrated*, the Army's letter specified that the training should be "in such tactics that would make better riders and enable them to perform many feats hitherto unknown to them." The Van Buren sisters were aware of these instructions from the War Department because they were active in motorcycle groups and regularly read the various motorcycle journals which carried these notices.

How very frustrating for them to want to perform those duties, be qualified to carry them out based on four years of what can only be described as advanced motorcycling experience, but not be included in the training and consideration even after what they had done to prove themselves.

In their home state, the 71st Regiment of the New York National Guard had formed a motorcycle battery. It saw service in the summer of 1916 along the Mexican border, and was mobilized in 1917 again for domestic duties protecting New York's infrastructure, such as harbors, water supplies, and important governmental facilities.

Motorcyclists themselves were anxious to do their part. Hundreds of riders across the country took part in specialized training at many army bases in preparation for possible mobilization. Famed racer Erwin "Cannon Ball" Baker himself trained prospective dispatch riders at Fort Benjamin Harrison near Indianapolis.

Motor Cycle Illustrated magazine took remarkable action just days before the United States entered the War in April 1917, with President Wilson's plea to Congress for "a crusade to make the world safe for democracy." It published "A Pledge of Loyalty," which it encouraged all 200,000 motorcyclists in the nation to sign and submit.

The pledge read:

> "Being fully aware of the vital import of the present national crisis, and of the immediate necessity for a frank voicing of sentiments, I hereby reaffirm my loyalty to the Government of the United States and pledge my willingness—as a motorcyclist—to devote myself and my machine to such service as may be required for the defense of the nation and the precious traditions for which it stands."

But even the *Motor Cycle Illustrated* editorial that encouraged signing the Loyalty Pledge made it clear that they were referring only to male riders. The emotional plea for patriotism by magazine editors ended with, "Now our day has come. Let us speak out—200,000 strong—and voice our loyalty and our willingness to do, when the colors call, all that a man may do."

THE VAN BUREN SISTERS knew they had a difficult challenge ahead of them, but that didn't deter them from trying. They would do all that they could to convince the country of the need to gear up for war, and they would do their utmost to demonstrate their abilities to assist in war time duties. If others failed to follow through, it would not be because the sisters hadn't given it their best shot.

It's pretty obvious that they hoped their actions would aid in another fight that was taking place in American society—the right for women to vote. They had heard the argument that, since women didn't serve in the military or fight in wars, they hadn't "earned" the right to vote. This logic was the source of great frustration because, when women such as Augusta and Adeline tried to join the military, they were turned down.

Joseph Heller's 1961 book *Catch-22* hadn't been published yet, so the idiom Catch 22—meaning being caught in an absurd no-win situation—was not yet in use. But American women who wished to serve their country in the military and to vote in its elections at the time of the First World War certainly found themselves in such a classic, no-win predicament.

ADDIE AND GUSSIE planned their 1916 cross-country trip in great detail, with an ambitious schedule that showed their level of confidence. Their initial plan called for leaving New York City on July 4 and arriving in San Francisco August 9, allowing some time for sightseeing followed by a leisurely train ride back to New York so that Adeline could resume her teaching duties in early September.

To make the 3,800-mile trip seem easier to accomplish, they viewed it as 35 individual rides of just over one hundred miles each. Over the previous three years, they had done countless rides of this length without major incident and thus felt it would be very possible to do 35 separate trips again on nearly consecutive days. They frequently told reporters that they viewed the trip on a 'one day at a time' basis right from the beginning. This made the undertaking seem much more feasible and less daunting than looking at it as one trip of nearly 4,000 miles.

The sisters chose July 4 as their departure date for more than the obvious patriotic connection. The Federation of American Motorcyclists' annual convention was in New York City that week, and a full slate of motorcycle racing was scheduled on Independence Day. The sisters thought that they could attend some FAM functions, watch the Federation-sanctioned professional motorcycle races, and still get out of town in the afternoon.

The races were to be held at one of the country's newest premier racing venues, and they did not want to miss the action. FAM's selection of New York as the site of their 1916 convention, and the several categories of races associated with the convention, resulted directly from actions taken two years earlier by local officials and business leaders.

In 1914 the Sheepshead Bay Speedway Corporation, which included many of the most successful entrepreneurs of the day, such as Carl Fisher of Indianapolis, among its investors, decided to build an automobile race course in New York City. The facility would be world class, equal to or better than the best tracks in America or Europe. The company bought the 400 acre site from the Coney Island Jockey Club. It had been a horse racing venue for many years, but horse racing in the state had fallen on hard times.

Work commenced at a feverish pace during 1915 to have the facility finished in time for auto races in October. The track, called a motordrome, was built in the Sheepshead Bay section of Brooklyn near Coney Island and was a marvel of engineering and design. The two-mile course was constructed of wood planks, the preferred race surface at the time as many felt that wood provided a faster surface than any other, and it could be built to exacting specifications. The wood was Long Leaf Georgia Pine, cut into 2x4s that were laid on edge to take advantage of the improved traction provided by the edge grain.

The track itself was seventy feet wide and, with banked curves 25 feet high, it could support speeds up to 125 miles per hour, with space for up to forty cars. Underground parking allowed 20,000 cars to be out of sight, and the massive seating area could accommodate an astonishing 175,000 spectators on concrete and steel bleachers.

The venue was also designed to host much more than just auto and motorcycle races. The infield was designed to be a level turf surface to allow golf, football, baseball, track events, and even polo matches. The developers also envisioned using the infield for aviation events since all wiring would be run in underground conduits.

It is no surprise, then, that the 1916 FAM convention was held in New York with sanctioned races at this marvelous new track. It was a bold move, however, as it meant that the competitions were scheduled for the same day as the famous Dodge City 300 where Harley-Davidson racer Floyd Clymer was to set two speed records that day.

Red Parkhurst, the first rider to sign on with the Harley-Davidson racing team, won both the 100-mile national event and the FAM National Professional Championship. In fact, Harley-Davidson, which had only gotten involved with racing in a serious manner in 1914 at regional races and at major national races in1915, won the first four places at Sheepshead Bay that day.

A series of state and local amateur races made the racing card an all-day affair for that pioneering event, and an estimated 18,000 people were on hand as cited in records at the American Motorcycle Association Museum. Among the thousands of screaming fans who watched the death defying antics of racers as they circled the track at breakneck speed were Adeline and Augusta Van Buren.

THEY WERE PROBABLY disappointed that an Indian rider didn't win either of the main races, but seeing Arthur Chapple take second place in the FAM Nationals aboard an Indian must have given Hendee boosters some consolation. All in all, the Van Buren sisters enjoyed a sunny afternoon filled to the brim with spectacular racing, and they were up late that evening enjoying the parties and related events that followed.

The race and associated activities lasted so long, and they so enjoyed themselves, that the sisters didn't embark on their journey that day, but chose to put it off until the next. This change in their ambitious schedule was but the first of many.

Whereas the sun had shined on New York for the races and other holiday activities on Tuesday, steady rains fell on July 5 as most people went back to their normal routines. Augusta and Adeline didn't leave New York City until 11:30 that Wednesday morning, hoping that the rain would eventually quit; it didn't. The Van Burens were sanguine about the precipitation. Adeline noted in a *Motorcycling and Bicycling* magazine article, that "a bad beginning should make a splendid finish."

The first alteration to the route they would follow also came that day. They had originally planned to ride from New York City to Schenectady, a distance of 165 miles. Instead, they rode in the rain from New York to Springfield, Massachusetts, to the factory where their 1916 Indian Powerplus motorcycles were made. This out-of-the-way trip may have been added at the last minute, perhaps at the request of the Hendee Manufacturing Company. The women probably regretted agreeing to the route change when they encountered three detours caused by rain-damaged roads between New York City and Springfield; not an auspicious way to start such a journey.

The Indian Powerplus was Hendee's top of the line model and represented the latest in technological advancements with a new and easier to use starter mechanism, 3-speed transmission, and an improved foot operated clutch. A sturdy chain transferred power to the rear wheel, rather than a leather belt such as many manufacturers used. To help smooth the ride a bit, rudimentary leaf springs were installed front and rear. The sisters' machines were also specially equipped with acetylene gas headlights. With standard 28-inch wheels it was a tall machine. The Indian Powerplus was regarded as a very dependable bike with 998 cubic centimeters (61 cubic inches) of V-twin power and torque to

A 1916 Indian Powerplus motorcycle, the same model as those ridden by the Van Buren sisters across America in 1916. (Photo by author)

move along at more than 60 miles per hour; if a road smooth enough to handle that speed could be found.

Riding fast on pre-World War I bikes came with a price, however. Most motorcycles, including the Powerplus, lacked a front brake, which provides the majority of stopping power on two-wheelers. The rear brake alone was pitifully inadequate for quick stops. Early motorcycles had a lot more ability to go than to stop; one sped at his or her own risk! The bike got its unusual name after a tester reportedly exclaimed "This thing has power plus!" They sold in 1916 for a base price of $275.

THE SISTERS WERE not subtle about their trip. Banners draped across the front of each machine declared Coast to Coast and New York to Frisco in large letters. Because publicity for their military and preparedness causes was a key part of the trip, the pair conducted many interviews throughout their 3,800 mile journey across the continent. Unlike the Hotchkisses, the Van Burens made it a point to stay in towns each night, and their arrival was often reported by local papers.

The ease and willingness with which the sisters spoke with reporters represented a significant change from just three years earlier. When they first began motorcycling, they complained of being viewed as curiosities and objects of wonderment. When a reporter telephoned to interview them, they refused to speak to him and hung up on the surprised caller. They soon learned, however, that speaking with reporters was the best method to get their message out to the largest number of people, and they became very skilled at the give and take of interviews.

In a lengthy interview with a reporter from the *Springfield Daily Republican* on the evening of their arrival, the sisters gave insight into the reasons for their trip and of their own roles. The published article noted that Adeline was a gifted mechanic. She was described as "the official machinist of the expedition, and she can cope with any of the ordinary problems which confront motorcyclists." She was also described as the "directing spirit" of the duo. Augusta, on the other hand, was cited as the team's navigator. It was she who had studied the system of roads across the country and who would make decisions about the best course to take while under way.

ON JULY 6 THE WOMEN rode on the Post Road that connected Boston and Albany, taking a new route over the Berkshire Mountains of western Massachusetts. The original road was a series of steep switchbacks that attacked the mountains head on and, for decades, was called "Jacob's Ladder." The source of the name is unclear, but it was a dangerous route that claimed many lives over the years.

The recently-opened bypass through the mountains was much gentler and more scenic and enjoyable. This new stretch of road built in 1910 was also paved with an early version of macadam, and a vast improvement over the rough, rocky dirt road it replaced.

The scenic byway quickly became an attraction in its own right. It was the first road in America built over a mountain range and was designed specifically for the burgeoning popularity of automobile travel and tourism. The route was officially designated as U.S. 20 a decade later. It is a popular scenic byway today, a beautiful and enjoyable ride. What a memorable start to their westward journey as the

The new road through the Berkshire Mountains of western Massachusetts eliminated a series of dangerously steep and rocky switchbacks. It immediately became a popular tourist attraction as autoists and motorcyclists traveled from cities such as New York, Albany, and Boston just for the chance to ride this new and improved road through the scenic mountains. (Photo by author)

riders flowed with the curves while their powerful engines smoothly propelled them up and over the forested slopes of the Berkshires.

A tradition that started shortly after 1910 was for tourists to bring a large stone, engraved with information about their home towns, and place it in a cairn at the highest point of the road where it crossed the mountains. For many years, the stones were moved around as new ones were added or lower ones were raised higher in the cairn. In 1946 the stones were finally cemented in place and the cairn exists yet today.

THE RIDERS MADE it all the way to Schenectady by the end of their second day. The following day found them in Buffalo at day's end, but not before being treated to lunch in Syracuse by The Olmstead Company—the local Indian Motorcycle agency—and the Syracuse Firestone dealer. Even with the stop in Syracuse, they rode more than three hundred miles across the state through the Mohawk Valley in just one day. This segment of road was the best they would ride.

The highway across New York had existed for generations and was well-traveled and maintained. It had started centuries before as an Indian trail, and was subsequently used by fur traders, explorers, European and American military units, and finally westbound immigrants in the 1800s. The Erie Canal, built in the 1820s, roughly paralleled the road, making the Mohawk Valley a critical link in America's westward expansion.

But even on this well-maintained road, the unpredictable happened. A horse, spooked by their machines, bumped into Augusta and forced her into a ditch. Neither rider nor machine was injured so, once things calmed down, the sisters were able to right her motorcycle and head west once again.

In Buffalo, the women were guests of Mr. Alvah Stratton, the local Indian motorcycle representative. They knew Mr. Stratton because he had been a racer in his earlier years, piloting Indians on tracks in the Northeast. Having Stratton as a local guide was a godsend for the sisters because, probably unbeknownst to them, Buffalo was hosting the 1916 national Shriners convention when the Van Burens arrived in town.

The Lafayette Hotel, where they probably intended to stay for the night, was filled to capacity. According to the *Buffalo Evening News*, tens of thousands of Shriners and their families and friends had filled every hotel room in the city and surrounding area! Stratton was probably very helpful in finding lodging for the road-weary women.

July 8 was a day of rest and recreation for the Van Buren sisters, so they saw the sights of Buffalo and took advantage of the Shriners' entertainment opportunities. They certainly didn't spend the day at Stratton's Indian agency, kicking tires and talking about the comparative strengths of various brands of machines. In addition to spectacular parades during daylight hours, several well-known theater and music troupes were performing for the Shriners in the evening, and these gregarious young ladies would have had a hard time resisting the temptation for a night on the town.

ADELINE DESCRIBED THE route between Buffalo and Erie, Pennsylvania, as an endurance run. She portrayed it as "deep, deep sand," and it was the first of many challenging miles that lay ahead. Once they got beyond Erie, the sand changed to dirt, but the dust was so bad that it permeated every nook and cranny of their gear and clothing. All in all, it was a difficult, hot day, especially considering the outfits they wore.

The women dressed in tan-colored leather from head to toe. Leather pants, heavy, knee-length leather coats, calf-high leather boots, thick leather gloves with long gauntlets, and the *de rigueur* leather helmet and goggles all provided protection from the elements and a cushion should they have an accident. However, the garments were exceedingly hot and uncomfortable. The women viewed their riding attire as the best that they could hope for. Adeline told a reporter from a motorcycling journal, "Each outfit looks well, is waterproof and will stand very hard usage. It is lighter than any khaki outfit made."

They arrived in Akron late in the day on July 10, taking a break in that city and visiting the Firestone Rubber Company tire factory the next day. They clearly enjoyed the guided tour they received at the sprawling facility and had kind words for the company and its product, which they were using on their machines.

The trip to Akron was a significant detour for them, but was likely an agreed-upon promotional stop. Today, that relatively short drive down I-77 to reach Akron wouldn't be too much of a burden, but in the day of dirt roads it was a significant investment of time and effort. The July 27, 1916, edition of *Motor Cycle Illustrated* headlined the story of their visit with "Van Buren Girls Warmly Welcomed in Tire City."

In her glowing report about Firestone tires Augusta said,

> "After seeing the care, the skillful workmanship and the quality materials put into Firestone tires and the high standard of the whole organization behind the Firestone products, we are now able to understand why our tires are giving us 'no-trouble' service over all kinds of roads."

The Firestone tires did perform extremely well. In an era where flats and blow outs were common, Augusta made the entire trip without a single tire repair, and Adeline had to patch only two punctures.

One tire had to be replaced on Adeline's machine, but that was because it rubbed against a water bag hung on the bike, not due to a flaw in the tire. They used the tire repair kits they carried primarily to help other travelers.

According to Goodyear Tire Company advertisements at that time, virtually all motorcycle manufacturers used Goodyear tires as standard equipment, so the fact that the Van Burens were using Firestone tires is significant. Although no official record of sponsorship exists, it is clear that Firestone provided logistical assistance.

All along their trip the sisters stopped at Firestone and Indian dealers, and a Firestone dealer in New York City displayed a large map in the front window of his store with updates on the women's current location, which they telegraphed or telephoned to him daily. These stops were photo-ops for the dealer and the women, and several photographs show the sisters parked in front of various storefronts.

In an interview upon the conclusion of their trip, Augusta noted that they had purchased the motorcycles they used on the journey, which meant that the factory had not provided them as part of a promotional opportunity.

Many daring trips of the day, especially those involving high-profile persons, had considerable advertising value for a sponsor or corporate brand name. The sisters' use of Firestone tires was a clear example of this mutually beneficial relationship. Firestone got tremendous good will from the sisters' successful trip on their tires, and the women benefitted from the knowledge that a Firestone outlet would provide help with their tires if necessary. The women displayed pennants with the words "Firestone Cycle Tires", and also used heavy duty canvas duffle bags with Firestone's name clearly printed on them.

As a result of their trip, the sisters had residual advertising value and benefits, for themselves and for the companies that manufactured their equipment. Using the Van Burens' names and photographs in advertisements of Indian motorcycles proved valuable to Hendee Manufacturing, and Firestone continued to benefit from their use of that company's tires.

In 1917 Prest-O-Lite Company advertisements featured the sisters in a photograph but did not mention them by name. Their bikes were equipped with Prest-O-Lite acetylene gas headlights, and that equipment's Indianapolis manufacturer made a clear connection between Augusta and Adeline's successful cross-country journey and the quality of their product.

Mr. Carl Fisher—one of the original forces behind the creation of the Lincoln Highway—was also a partner and primary driving force in the Prest-O-Lite Company. That company convinced automobile and motorcycle manufacturers to put lights on vehicles, thus making night travel possible, although not recommended!

From 1905 to just after the First World War Prest-O-Lite gas headlights were standard equipment on most vehicles, making Fisher and his partners millionaires very quickly. Eventually, electrical technology on motorized vehicles evolved to the point that electrically-powered bulbs could provide reliable lighting, and the bulky acetylene tanks and lamps were finally replaced by lightweight, safer, electrical components.

THE VAN BURENS were stoic when describing their trip thus far to Akron reporters. Augusta said in passing that they had "had a few spills" but that all was well and riders and machines were doing fine. After spending two days in Akron, they arrived on July 13 in Toledo, where, as reported by the *Toledo News Bee*, they visited the Toledo Tire & Supply Company—the local Firestone dealer—and the Union Supply Company, Toledo's Indian agency.

Joining the Lincoln Highway near the small, western Ohio town of Bryan, they rode across northern Indiana toward Chicago. They sent postcards back home from Ligonier, Indiana, on July 14 and were in Chicago the following evening.

The short article in the Sunday *Chicago Tribune* on July 16 had the headline "Two Girls, Attired as Men, Travel on Motorcycles." The story went on to explain that the "young society women" were attempting to prove that women were able to serve as dispatch riders, but the headlines told the "real" story as viewed by the paper's editors. Even in a cosmopolitan city such as Chicago, the story was less about their efforts toward military preparedness and the role of women in the military than two girls dressed like men were riding motorcycles.

Their ride across Ohio and Indiana was not without incident. The women encountered severe thunderstorms, and the roads had turned to greasy mud. These conditions resulted in several spills, but they simply got their machines upright again, without help, and continued down the road in the rain and the muck. One day they did seek refuge at a farmhouse during a particularly bad thunderstorm.

The bad weather and impassable roads in the Midwest were having far-reaching repercussions. Ohio National Guard units had been called up for service along the Mexican border during the summer of 1916. They went through final training at Camp Willis near Columbus, but when the day came to move out, they couldn't. The roads leading south from Columbus were impassable. Akron newspapers declared that "Heavy Rains have Cut off Supply Train" and "Held up at Columbus Because of Muddy Conditions of Roads."

Residents of the Midwest and Plains states are well aware of the powerful storms that sweep across the region in the spring and summer months. Nowadays, motorcyclists are likely to seek shelter at various places--expressway overpasses, park picnic shelters, or gas stations; anywhere that they can find a safe haven. Riders a century ago had no such escape. They motored on through the deluge and the slippery mud until they could find refuge in a farmhouse or barn. Many would have sought shelter under a large roadside tree, but using such a sanctuary in thunderstorms carried its own potential price tag, being struck by lightning!

Every article by men and women who endured these conditions while traveling during that period was written in an understated, matter-of-fact style. They did not exaggerate, did not belabor the point of bad roads, did not go into great detail about accidents or spills caused by the mud and rain. They simply reported that they had "had a few spills" or that the condition of the roads was "muddy."

The reality was worse than the intrepid women let on. They later told family members that they were often so tired from struggling through the muddy conditions that they sometimes fell asleep while riding, falling over into the mud. Today these spills would almost certainly result in an ambulance and police response, but hardy riders in those days simply picked themselves up, straightened whatever might have bent, got back on their bikes and continued down the muddy trail. North American road conditions as late as 1916 were such that the *Chicago Tribune* felt it newsworthy to report on July 5 that "two Canadian autoists, from Winnipeg and Toronto, arrived in Chicago."

THE SISTERS SPENT a couple of days seeing the sights of the Windy City, which naturally included a stop at the local Indian dealer, and then proceeded west again on the Lincoln Highway. They arrived in Dixon, Illinois, on July 19. Dixon is noteworthy because several previous travelers reported that, from Dixon westward, the road was notorious for being in bad condition, with ruts during dry periods and deep mud when it rained. They slowly crossed Illinois without serious incident on a stretch of the Lincoln Highway that Chicago newspapers reported as being muddy. This was surely an understatement because pictures of that portion of the highway show deep ruts with standing water.

Photographs of the Van Burens' motorcycles show mud guards that protected both the engine and the women from stones and mud thrown back by the front wheel. They were installed once under way, as pictures taken at the beginning of the trip don't show them. The well-designed shields made a great improvement in dealing with the mud and loose gravel they encountered. They didn't make negotiating the mud any easier, but at least less of it wound up on the women. The devices also prevented damage to the engine from flying stones and reduced the likelihood of dirt entering the carburetion system, while strategically placed louvers in the guards allowed adequate air movement to keep the air-cooled engines from overheating.

Augusta and Adeline crossed the Mississippi River over the Lyons Bridge at Clinton, Iowa, and continued slowly westward across the rolling farmland of America's heartland to Ames. From there they took the Jefferson Highway—a series of dirt roads between Winnipeg, Manitoba, and New Orleans—to their next stop...Des Moines. They stayed the night of July 22 in the stylish Chamberlain Hotel (touted in advertisements as the newest, best, and positively fireproof) in downtown Des Moines and spent the next day going about the city.

But any celebratory mood the sisters experienced in Des Moines would have been shattered as they read accounts in the local newspapers of the July 22 bombing at the Preparedness Day Parade in San

The Chamberlain Hotel, formerly located on Locust Street in downtown Des Moines, represented the latest in hotel style and technology. It was in community gathering places such as this that Adeline and Augusta met with local reporters and citizens to talk about Preparedness. (Photo used by permission of Drake University Library)

Francisco. This cause was very close to their hearts, so reading of the anarchists' bombing, and of the many resulting fatalities and injuries, would have been heart-breaking. The incident also unquestionably hardened their resolve to spread the preparedness message during the remainder of their trip.

Their confidence in getting to the West Coast close to schedule was still fairly high. They now told reporters that they anticipated arriving in San Francisco on August 15. This was six days later than their original goal, but, they had encountered terrible roads in the more than 1,000 miles they had ridden thus far, so they weren't unduly concerned about being behind schedule less than a week. It would also be logical to assume that, as one rode west, the roads would be dryer and the rain less frequent, making riding conditions more favorable. They could hope to make up the time on roads in the West.

UNFORTUNATE LUCK brought the Van Burens to Iowa in the middle of a record-breaking heat wave. The newspaper headlines glumly reported that the entire month of July had seen abnormally hot weather, with more to come for the foreseeable future. The head-to-toe leather garb that Addie and Gussie wore must have been on the verge of unbearable in the city heat, and they were probably anxious to continue their trip if only to cool off in the wind of the road.

July 24 found them riding across western Iowa on the River-To-River Road toward Council Bluffs and the Missouri River in temperatures approaching 100°. West of Des Moines, other motorcyclists joined them as they and a local motorcycle policeman led quite the parade to Council Bluffs and across the river into Omaha, Nebraska.

In Omaha, the women stopped at the Omaha Bicycle Company, the Indian motorcycle agency. At the garage, they had their machines' suspension and frame lowered so that they could reach the ground with their feet when sitting in the saddle. Lowering the level of the seat would have made the machines more comfortable and significantly easier to handle in the rough conditions they were encountering. Both of them were quite short. Adeline was a mere 5 feet 2 inches tall and weighed only 105 pounds. Augusta was a bit taller but still a poor match for the ergonomics of the standard motorcycle of that era.

The owners of the Omaha Indian shop also gave the women a .32 caliber handgun to carry with them for their protection. Perhaps it was meant as a present for Adeline to mark her 27th birthday, which fell on July 26. Neither Adeline nor Augusta felt they needed a weapon and put it in the bottom of a duffle bag where it remained unused through the end of their trip.

For several days the women followed the Lincoln Highway through the wide open landscape between Omaha and Denver. The weather was hot and dry, and the roads across the Great Plains were dusty but passable. In Ogallala, Nebraska they left the main branch of the Lincoln Highway and rode southwest on what was called the "Denver Loop" of the Lincoln, through Sterling, Colorado, and on to Greeley and Denver.

It was in Denver that the women would have heard about the massive explosion on Black Tom Island near their New York City home. The small island was the site of a large ammunition depot and was a loading point for munitions bound for the Allies in Europe. On July 30 German agents sabotaged the depot, causing a massive explosion that destroyed the facility and killed at least four people. Metal fragments struck the Statue of Liberty, causing significant damage. Shrapnel also hit buildings in Jersey City, a mile away. War had struck very close to their homes, and this event would certainly have solidified their commitment to the mission of preaching the need for preparedness.

BECAUSE OF BAD weather delays, the Van Burens were running at least a week behind their original schedule by the time they reached Denver. They had left adequate time at the end of their trip to make it back to New York for their work duties, and perhaps they were not yet feeling any pressure from falling behind.

The bikers enjoyed a break as guests of the Boyd & Williams Indian Agency in Denver, resting and touring the city. They then rode the rough and rocky trail south to Colorado Springs where they spent more time seeing the sights, including stops at Seven Falls Canyon and the Manitou Cliff Dwellings. An August 6 telegraph sent from Colorado Springs to their home assured their family they were doing fine and were in no trouble, though they did mention the muddy roads and bad weather they had experienced.

Their most noteworthy accomplishment in Colorado Springs, however, was riding their bikes to the top of Pikes Peak on the newly opened Pikes Peak Highway. Spencer Penrose, a Colorado man who had made his fortune in the Cripple Creek gold mining boom of the late 1800s, realized the economic potential of tourism and wanted to make it possible for individuals to drive their automobiles to the top of the mountain. A carriage road to the summit had existed for nearly thirty years, but it was a crude and narrow trail up the mountainside, suitable only for horses. Penrose envisioned an improved version on which cars could safely, and relatively easily, ascend the iconic peak.

With a permit from the U.S. Agriculture Department, which had the responsibility to manage America's newly established national forest lands, and $500,000 in financial backing, he began construction in 1914 and finished upgrading the old carriage road in 1915. Immediately, the mountain became an attraction in its own right, with people going to Colorado solely for the purpose of driving their vehicle to the top of Pikes Peak and acquiring the bragging rights that went with that accomplishment.

The Van Buren sisters had almost certainly read of this new road and decided, while planning their trip, to climb the mountain. Making the long and difficult detour south from the Lincoln Highway to Colorado Springs was a very significant investment of time and effort, and they would have done it only for a high priority reason. On August 5

Pikes Peak looms in the background. The barren wind-swept peak is the goal of thousands of drivers who accept the challenges presented by the narrow dirt road leading to the top. Though much of the road has been paved, large dirt and stone segments remain, to test the nerve of modern day tourists. (Photo by author)

they rode their machines to the top, thus becoming the first women to ride their own motorcycles to the summit of this famous mountain.

A number of stories about this event have been published in latter day magazines, books, newsletters, and Internet sites, but many of them incorrectly claim a variety of "firsts" for the women. They were not the first people to ride a motorized vehicle of any kind to the summit nor did they even claim to be the first motorcyclists to ride the road to the top of the peak.

In fact, two men from Denver drove the first motorized vehicle to the top of Pikes Peak in 1901, when they took their twin-cylinder steam powered Locomobile up the old carriage road. Prior to that—actually since 1889—tourists had been going to the top of the mountain in horse drawn carriages. The feeble Locomobile took over nine hours to reach the summit and required the passenger to get out and push in some places. It was an amusing sight for teamsters guiding

horse-drawn carriages up the slope whenever they passed the horseless
carriage. It would have been a reassurance to horse and man alike that
these noisy and smelly contraptions would never replace the trusty
flesh and blood steed, and the men who guided them.

Floyd Clymer, famed motorcycle and car racer, was reportedly the
first to ascend the mountain on a motorcycle, also on the old carriage
road, circa 1910. However, although not so famous as Clymer, Messrs.
Sheff and Riggs of nearby Colorado Springs also rode their cycles to
the top during this period, possibly in 1909.

The new road was ready for business in early summer of 1916,
having been open for some time before the sisters rode to the top on
August 5, and many cars and motorcycles had ascended the peak during the interim. But the Van Buren sisters were the first women to ride
to the 14,110 foot summit on their own machines.

This was no run-of-the-mill feat! The road was rough and muddy
and required great skill. It is a challenging ride today on a motorcycle;
in 1916 it would have been a very demanding undertaking. To make
matters worse for the ladies, a fierce thunderstorm hit the mountain
the day before their ascent. This storm left the road in even worse
condition than usual. Tragically, a road worker was killed in the storm
when he was hit by lightning just hours before the sisters reached
the summit.

The riders were very proud of their Pikes Peak accomplishment,
but, in their usual understated manner of speaking, they played down
the degree of difficulty. On August 6 Adeline told the reporter from
the Colorado Springs newspaper,

> "We didn't really feel that we had achieved anything wonder-
> ful until yesterday. ...we did not really become elated until we
> mounted Pikes Peak. Now we know we have really done a
> wonderful thing. Why, we fairly raced away from the automo-
> biles and motor buses, both going and coming, and we didn't
> have to dismount once."

Having also ridden to the top of Pikes Peak on a motorcycle immediately following a heavy rainstorm, I know that Adeline was being very
modest in her description of their ride. Even though I encountered sig-

nificantly fewer miles of dirt roadway when I went up in 2010, muddy road conditions made for a thrilling ride with no room for errors!

The timing of the Van Buren sisters' ride was perfect. They were departing Colorado Springs just as thousands of racing enthusiasts were pouring into town from across North America. The event was the first ever Pikes Peak Road Race. It was billed as the longest and highest hill climbing course on the planet. All hotel rooms were filled, and people were finding it difficult to find places to park their cars and motorcycles. It was the largest event ever to hit the area, and dozens of men were deputized to maintain order.

Some of the best known auto and motorcycle racers in America, including men such as Barney Oldfield and future ace military pilot Eddie Rickenbacker, were competing for the Penrose Cup, and the prize monies that came to those who completed the perilous race at high speeds ahead of other drivers. The road consisted of dozens of unprotected hairpin curves as it climbed the steep mountainside. Losing control on one of these curves meant plummeting hundreds of feet to a certain death. A relatively unknown driver by the name of Rea Lentz won the automobile race, taking home the substantial first-place prize of $2,000 for his troubles.

Four classes of motorcycle races took place on August 10, the first day of the three-day racing marathon. Floyd Clymer won both professional races on an Excelsior motorcycle in that original "Race to the Clouds" event. The race has taken place annually ever since, with the exception of certain war years, including the 1917 races that were cancelled due to America's entry into World War I. It continues to draw the best racers from around the world.

To ADD TO THE congestion and bustle in Colorado Springs during the Pikes Peak races, the National Woman's Party also held its annual convention there that week. And, like the racers and thousands of spectators, the mountain itself played a major role. The women used the summit to attract attention to the suffrage movement by staging a large demonstration and flag-raising. Thirty women drove to the top, installed a large flagpole and also raised a large banner to publicize what was being called the "Susan B. Anthony Amendment;" the proposed 19th amendment to the U.S. Constitution. The proposal wasn't fully adopted for four more years, but the Pikes Peak demonstration was one more step in the long upward march to secure women's right to vote.

THE SISTERS COULDN'T have known then that their time in Colorado Springs was to mark the highlight of their trip, and that the next three weeks would test their resolve and abilities to the extreme. They had no way of knowing what that vast expanse of rugged wilderness between the front face of the Rockies and the Sierra Nevada Mountains of California held in store for them.

Their original itinerary called for them to depart Colorado Springs to the north, going back through Denver and north to Cheyenne and the Lincoln Highway once again. It appears that, at this point, they decided to go west over the mountains rather than north to Wyoming.

The women followed a frontier path called the Midland Trail through the heart of the Rocky Mountains (roughly the same route as today's U.S. 24), over Ute Pass, through Leadville, Glenwood Canyon, and ultimately Grand Junction in western Colorado on the eastern edge of the inhospitable Great Basin. The Midland Trail was a narrow, rocky path cut through the mountains, very unlike the smooth ribbons of pavement that we drive through the Rockies on today.

West of Colorado Springs, the women encountered heavy rain storms and road conditions that could only be described as terrible. Near Gilman conditions became impassable despite their determined efforts. They were forced to abandon their machines in the deep mud and hike the muddy trail into the remote mining town for help. At an altitude of 9,000 feet the conditions were not only wet and muddy, they were wet and cold.

What a sight it must have been, and what a look of surprise would have crossed the faces of the rough and tumble miners when these two young women, dressed head to toe in leather, walked out of the gloom into the sodden village on that dreary day. They immediately won the respect and support of the townspeople and a group of miners went back with the women to help extricate their motorcycles from the mud. After much effort, riders and machines were once again under way on the muddy trail.

It took them five days to get through the heart of the mountains, arriving in Grand Junction on August 11. Grand Junction might have been the key to their changed plans. Mr. W.M. Van Buren, a relative of theirs, lived there. Perhaps they decided at the last minute to take advantage of the opportunity to visit him and his family and altered their plans accordingly.

THEY RELAXED A BIT in Grand Junction, spending the night of August 11 at the La Court Hotel and lunching the next day at the home of their Van Buren relatives. The week of August 6, 1916, was "National Touring Week," a part of the "See America First" campaign. On August 12 the sisters had their picture taken in front of the city's Peter Fox Indian Agency. In the background was a large banner proclaiming "National Touring Week," along with advertising displays for Thor and Indian motorcycles.

Heavy rains in Grand Junction caused them to spend three days there, putting them further behind schedule. Feeling the need to move on, the sisters rode west into Utah toward the small town of Price. What should have been a relatively easy one- or two-day trip took five days due to abominable road conditions, "unspeakably bad" in the words of the normally sanguine Adeline.

The *Grand Junction Daily Sentinel* reported on the terrible weather that the two transcontinentalists had experienced firsthand. Headlines on August 4, 1916, proclaimed: "Cloudburst washes out 4 bridges; Western Slope visited by Heavy Rainstorm." But the storms didn't end after just a day or two; a series of powerful thunderstorms hit the area for days on end in August that year. The damage to the roads would take months to repair, not to mention numerous mud and rock slides that also impacted the ability to travel safely throughout the central Rockies.

Deep mud and unrelenting rain would have been enough to test the resolve of anyone, but simply being able to find and stay on the correct trail was a challenge in itself. It was a far cry from a drive today on U.S. 6—the well marked paved road that closely follows the path of the original unsigned trail through that region.

They arrived at the isolated village of Price on August18 and, as you might imagine, made quite an impression. It was much more normal to see a freight wagon pulled by mules coming into this small town than someone on a motorcycle, let alone two young women riding alone through those extreme conditions. The *Carbon County News Advocate* reported briefly on their trip and, in the manner of people living in the harsh conditions of this region where life had always been a struggle against the elements, noted simply, "They bore the marks of a hard journey."

The normally optimistic and positive Adeline later told a Salt Lake City reporter that "the roads were simply terrible from Grand Junction to Price." This was about as strong an indictment of the road conditions that one could get from these indomitable explorers. Even at this point, the sisters reported that they planned to reach San Francisco by August 28—more than two weeks off their original goal, but still with just enough time to allow them to get back to New York by September 5—Adeline's first day back to school.

They arrived in Salt Lake City on August 21, paid a courtesy call on the Lon Claflin Indian agency, and spent a restful night at the downtown Newhouse Hotel. A brief article in the *Salt Lake Telegram* reported that the women were dressed in "male garb" and that they "attracted some attention" at the Newhouse.

No doubt they did! The Newhouse was a very fashionable hotel favored by wealthy travelers and businessmen who would have been parading about the lobby in sartorial splendor. Seeing these two young women pull up in front of the hotel on their mud-encrusted motorcycles and make their dramatic entrance with muddy boots and soiled leather "male garb" would certainly have caused quite a stir. It was not a common sight in the socially conservative climate of Salt Lake City a century ago, so it's easy to picture the looks of shock and disapproval on the faces of the prim and proper society ladies on the arms of their nattily dressed husbands.

The *Telegram* article is the first report in which the sisters themselves described how and where they spent their nights while on the road. As Adeline reported, "We have put up at hotels and wayside inns every night, and have had many most delightful experiences." Given the underlying purpose of their trip, it would have been counterproductive for them to be reclusive. They wanted to interact with local residents, and one of the best ways to do this was at the downtown hotels they found in virtually every city and town.

It is easy to imagine the conversations. The women would have handed out Preparedness Movement literature and discussed the state of world affairs with local residents who were understandably myopic in their concerns; more worried about current grain or beef prices than what was happening across the Atlantic.

The Van Burens were intelligent professionals who were very capable of holding their own in any discussion about politics or international affairs. They made good impressions everywhere they went. The Grand Junction, Colorado, *Daily Sentinel* described them as "pretty, refined, and altogether charming."

While they were in Salt Lake City, Augusta and Adeline came to realize that they were not going to make it back to New York by the start of the new school year. Several days earlier in Price they had told a reporter that they planned to be in San Francisco by August 28, but they admitted in a Salt Lake City interview that they hoped to make it to San Francisco "in about ten days"—on or about Septem-ber 2—which would have made it almost impossible to get back to New York City on time. Adeline's deadline for returning to her teaching duties on September 5 was firm.

They could have decided to end their journey in Salt Lake City and take the train east from there so as to return by their original deadline, but they decided to continue west to the coast as planned. While in Salt Lake City, Adeline may well have used one of the new long distance phone lines that now connected that city with New York to telephone her family and the New York school system to inform them of the delay.

THE SISTERS LEFT Salt Lake City via the Lincoln Highway, which ran southwest from the city, south of Great Salt Lake, across the vast desert to Ely, Nevada, then west to Reno. History was close at hand on this part of the ride. The Lincoln Highway in western Utah and much of Nevada followed the old Pony Express Trail.

This expanse of barren desert represented the most dangerous portion of a trip across the country, especially in the dead of summer with oppressive heat and few places where one could find water, food, and gasoline. Even today, signs warn that services are a hundred miles apart. A hundred years ago, the distances were even greater and the chances of meeting other people on the road much slimmer.

It seemed that the Van Burens couldn't get a break from the weather. They encountered extreme conditions for the majority of their trip west of Akron, Ohio—record-setting heat and heavy rains. In the desert, the heat once again challenged them. Newspapers across the country took notice of the unusual heat wave that summer and the impact it was having on people, crops, and life in general almost everywhere. Though severe rainstorms soaked Colorado, crops were withering and forests burning because of drought conditions in other parts of the West.

Headlines in the *Wyoming Tribune* proclaimed "Sun Glares Mercilessly as Gotham Children Die." Forest fires raging across Canada killed 200 destroying entire remote towns. The July 31 *Chicago Tribune* reported, "Elephants Crazed by Heat Break Up Street Parade in LaGrange, Indiana." Seven elephants broke loose in 102-degree heat and rampaged through town in an attempt to find shade and water. Record heat killed 115 people on July 30 in Chicago, and 16 died in Gary, Indiana, where it was 116° that day.

Crops were withering and forests were burning in much of the West due to drought conditions. Localized violent storms caused flash floods in the southeastern United States killing scores of people. It was a summer of violent weather, and the sisters rode their Indians through the worst of it as they worked their way west with no thought of stopping or seeking alternative transportation.

EVEN IN THE most rural portions of the country east of Salt Lake City, a farm or small town was never too far away. Help was within a reasonable walk or would eventually show up on its own if a person just waited patiently alongside the road. One did not need to carry several days' worth of water, gasoline, or food because outposts provided opportunities to replenish such necessities. This was especially important to the Van Burens because their ability to carry extra supplies was greatly limited; their motorcycles simply could not carry the same amount of gear and supplies as the Model Ts or Packards they occasionally encountered.

However, this safety net disappeared in central and western Utah. The salty land southwest of Utah's Great Salt Lake was only the beginning of the Great American Desert, which stretched all the way to the Sierra Nevada Mountains. The desert was a barren land of salt pans, sand, and stony hills that have an otherworldly look and feel. In this land of windswept sand and salt trails can completely disappear, while others that haven't been used in years appear freshly trod.

The women had been warned about this vast area that had changed little from the days of wagon trains and Pony Express riders. Early tourist guides and maps, as well as local residents living to the east of the desert, provided notice to travelers about the unique problems and dangers they would encounter in the vast salt flats southwest of Salt Lake City and the namesake lake.

Once beyond the small town of Tooele, the first stop for most drivers was at Orr's Ranch in Skull Valley. It was here that a person could replenish supplies, get water, and spend the night if necessary before venturing into the most remote portions of the enormous desert.

The *Nevada State Journal* even ran stories on where gasoline could be found in that immense area between Reno and Salt Lake City. A 1915 article reported that, once west of Salt Lake City, gas was usually available at Grantsville, 40 miles to the west. Beyond Grantsville, it was 30 miles to the Kanaka Ranch where one might find gasoline for purchase, and it was one hundred more miles of desolate scrub land until one reached a supply station at Fish Springs.

Gas wasn't a certainty at any of these remote outposts. One took a big chance that someone would be at the ranch or outpost, and that gas would be available. The paper also warned that "plenty of water, for drink and for the radiator, should be carried." It reported that water was available at Fish Springs.

However, west of the springs, it was over 140 miles on the Lincoln Highway to Ely, Nevada, the next oasis of civilization. The newspaper painted a depressing picture for continuing on to Reno. It described the 330-mile trip as having "bad turns, difficult crossings, and rocky grades." And this story was meant to be an upbeat report to let autoists know that it was possible, with just a bit of luck and care, to make the drive from Salt Lake City to Reno along the Lincoln Highway, so why not give it a try?

Many travelers dreaded this stretch of the Lincoln Highway the most, and with good reason. Many a tourist became lost or hopelessly mired in muddy salt pans after a rain. Entering the desert, one was welcomed by a sign advising people who were stranded to light a large bonfire of sage brush should they get lost or stuck, so that a rancher who lived in the area might see it and come to their aid.

The desert is so large and so remote that the U.S. Army chose it for testing chemical and biological weapons. The huge Dugway Proving Grounds was created early in World War II as a place where research and tests could be conducted without fear of affecting local populations. In 1916 the Lincoln Highway ran through this wide open, undeveloped space.

THE GREAT DESERTS of the American West have never discriminated in their utter lack of concern for the welfare of people who dare to cross their hot sands. Rich or poor, young or old, experienced or naïve, the desert doesn't care. Making mistakes can easily mean forfeiting one's life with no second chance and no appeals to a higher authority. Such has been the reality, the death-defying pact between desert and traveler, since time immemorial.

And so it seemed to Adeline and Augusta for a time. As the trail they had been following for nearly eighty miles gradually vanished in the desert, the sisters could see nothing but empty horizons and barren vistas in every direction they gazed. Sweltering heat accented a landscape of sand and crusted salt plains between the lifeless-looking hills that defined the valley.

Atmospheric waves caused by midday temperatures exceeding 100° only heightened the sense of being lost in an alien and inhospitable environment. After several false starts on trails that led nowhere, the unpleasant sensation of being hopelessly lost and in a precarious situation eventually settled on them like a heavy weight. They were out of water and would soon deplete what little gasoline remained in their tanks.

Despite all the difficulties they had faced thus far—recurrent storms, roads of deep greasy mud, spills and falls—this situation was the gravest in which they found themselves in the 2,000 miles they had ridden. The .32-caliber handgun that concerned Omaha Indian motorcycle dealer workers gave them for their safety would be of no value in this situation.

So it was, in a desolate region that early explorers and settlers had named Skull Valley that the sisters pondered their next move, knowing that whatever they decided would be vitally important. In considering their options, the women would have arrived at a sobering conclusion. They had no idea which direction to take to reach civilization, and they did not have enough gasoline to make repeated attempts should their first one fail. Moreover, they knew that the odds of a seeing another traveler at their remote location far from a main trail were extremely low. It was a truly desperate moment of emotional distress as they stopped to consider their options under an endless and beautiful, but utterly indifferent, sky.

IN WHAT SURELY seemed like a miracle to the women, their rescue came in an unlikely form. A prospector, still hoping to strike it rich in the Great Divide, appeared on the horizon, moving slowly toward them in his horse-drawn wagon. They must have seemed a strange apparition to him, every bit as much as he must have looked like an unlikely knight on a white horse to them.

Surely, never in the prospector's life had he experienced anything like it as he plodded along in the immense desert. And the sisters were probably never so happy to see another human being in such a remote location. The modern day Don Quixote provided the women with water and directions, and they continued on their separate ways. The sisters were able to resume their journey, with one more fascinating story to tell to family and friends once they made it safely back home.

The ride across Nevada was a hot and desolate exercise for the leather-clad Van Burens. The Lincoln Highway in Nevada used the existing Overland wagon train and stagecoach Trail, and very little had changed in the few years since pioneers plodded across it on their journeys to California and Oregon.

The trip across the Silver State was also a lesson in the politics of highways in that era.

A NEVADA GROUP wanted to replace the Lincoln Highway, which went straight west from Ely to Reno and ultimately to San Francisco (roughly today's U.S.50 route), with a route that went from Ely southwest to Tonapah and eventually to Los Angeles (the alignment of Route U.S. 6).

The Van Burens reported to the *Nevada State Journal* that many people in the Ely area were telling outrageous stories about the condition of the Lincoln Highway between Ely and Reno, trying to discourage people from risking it, and encouraging them to take their preferred route southwest instead. The Ely lobbyists claimed that the road in the vicinity of Fallon, just east of Reno, was in particularly bad condition and that it must be avoided.

But the riders on their iron horses successfully traversed the Lincoln Highway across Nevada without incident. When they reached Fallon, something seemed amiss. The desert was blooming and crops were growing where sand and salt should have prevailed. Just a generation earlier, the area near present-day Fallon was more infamous as the location of the 40-Mile Desert, a particularly desolate tract of land that presented a formidable barrier to settlers on their way to California. It was a large area devoid of water, and travelers had to carry enough of the precious commodity to get them and their horses or oxen to the Truckee River.

In 1916 Fallon was a new town built to serve an oasis of green created by a water diversion project completed a few years earlier. Water from the Truckee River had been diverted as part of a reclamation program enacted by Congress in 1902. That law changed the face of the West and resulted in many dams being built and irrigation projects installed throughout the arid region. Even today, the Fallon vicinity shows clear evidence of the old irrigation network, though the desert isn't quite as green as it once was.

Upon finally arriving in Reno, the hot, tired, and dusty riders spent a night at the Hotel Golden. One can imagine their relief at finding a place where they could enjoy all the amenities of a modern hotel in a city that was already famous for its night life.

THE TRIP OVER Donner Pass and across California was anti-climactic. The Van Burens encountered no problems and found the state's roads to be among the best they had ridden thus far. So they rode at a leisurely pace through the vineyards, orchards, and fruit farms of California's fertile Central Valley toward Oakland.

A representative from the Firestone Tire dealer Lausten & Ellis met the triumphant riders in Oakland, essentially marking the emotional end of their long road trip. The Firestone dealer confessed that he was so interested in the excellent condition of their tires that he failed to show proper courtesies to the sisters. They arrived in San Francisco Saturday, September 2, taking a ferry across the bay from Oakland.

Several newspaper and magazine articles reported on the sisters' arrival, but unfortunately no one was there to greet them as they rode off the ferry onto the streets of San Francisco at long last. Perhaps they had had a breakdown in communications or perhaps a last minute change in their expected arrival date might explain why the local Indian and Firestone dealers and fellow motorcyclists weren't on hand to welcome and escort them.

The women had held up their end of the business and promotional side of the trip. They had met with local dealers all the way across the continent, showing up for photo-ops and providing sincere testimony as to the worth of Indian motorcycles and Firestone tires. The welcome of fellow motorcyclists was foremost in their mind upon completing the trip, and their absence was most disappointing.

NEWSPAPERS FROM across the nation, as well as motorcycle journals, noted the completion of their journey with high praise. The *Syracuse Herald* was typical. In one rare article that used the word "women" rather than "girls" when describing their adventure, the paper used the following headline: "After Many Hardships New York Women End Cycle Trip to the Coast." The story went on to say,

"Impossible roads, unseasonable weather and difficulties in untold numbers were encountered at every turn. Washouts, mountain slides, desert wastes and wrecked bridges delayed but did not deter them. Incessant rains in Colorado made riding conditions the worst imaginable. Those days were followed by an equally arduous week in crossing the great American desert in Western Utah."

Some stories stated that they were in the desert for eleven days. Other newspaper articles reported that they had lost fifteen days of

Smooth roads and dry weather greeted the sisters upon their arrival in California, after enduring 3,000 miles of poor roads and stormy weather. (Photo used with permission of the Van Buren Family)

travel time because the road or storm conditions were so severe that they could not proceed.

It was obvious that the Van Buren sisters had earned the respect and admiration of the country, and especially of the doubters who felt they could never achieve what they set out to do. Augusta concisely summed up their feelings when she told a west coast reporter "Woman can, if she will." They had set out to prove a point and they succeeded. They also wanted to make it clear that it wasn't just an accomplishment for them; it was for all women.

WITH THE PRESSURE of having to be back in New York City before September 5 removed, the ladies decided to have some fun and take advantage of the great California weather and decent roads. Perhaps still stinging a bit from the lack of any significant welcome in San Francisco, they departed the city that Augusta cheekily called "this

The sisters were honored guests at the Panama-California Exposition held in San Diego's Balboa Park. The exposition celebrated southern California's Native American and Spanish heritage, in addition to the city's newfound economic status resulting from the opening of the Panama Canal. (Photo used with permission of the Van Buren family)

hick town" and headed south to Los Angeles and San Diego. There they were met by Mr. G. A. Davidson, president of the San Diego Exposition—a large fair meant to compete with the 1915 Panama-Pacific Exposition in San Francisco—who presented them with a special medal commemorating their trip.

From there, they decided to ride across the Mexican border into the bustling city of Tijuana, and newspapers reported that they were well received there. A warm reception in Mexico was not a given. Entering that country at the peak of the hostilities between the U.S. Army, the Mexican Army, and thousands of revolutionary rebels was a potentially very risky move. However, typical of their self-assurance and a basic trust in humanity, they crossed the border with a positive attitude and likely impressed everyone they met.

Despite potential dangers resulting from the violent revolution taking place in Mexico, Adeline and Augusta crossed the border to visit the bustling city of Tijuana. They experienced no troubles in their short venture into Mexican territory. (Photo used with permission of the Van Buren family)

Augusta and Adeline then rode back to Los Angeles where local Indian and Firestone dealers took them under their wing and showed them a great time. The sisters dined at some of the nicest restaurants in the area, saw many famous sites, and sailed out to Catalina Island. In what may have been one of the highlights of the trip, they met movie star Anita King, who had driven a car from California to New York the year before as a promotional event for Paramount Pictures. They visited the Hollywood studios and were even filmed in a small part by the Hearst-International movie company.

THE LOS ANGELES Indian agency helped load their well-worn machines on a train for the trip back home to New York. The machines had certainly earned a respite after their trouble free journey of over 5,000 miles through some of the worst conditions imaginable. On

The sisters charmed Hollywood with their style and grace. While at Paramount studios they met actress and fellow adventurer Anita King, who had driven a car across the continent the previous year. (Photo used with permission of the Van Buren family)

September 18, the women boarded a Southern Pacific Railway train for a leisurely trip that was to include stops at the Grand Canyon, New Orleans, and Washington, D.C. on their way back to their normal lives in New York City. How unusual it must have been for them to watch the landscape fly by from the comfort of their Pullman car. I wonder if they wished that they were back on their bikes and part of the action, rather than spectators.

One of the more baffling stories that resulted from the Van Burens' ride is a statement in a 1978 *Ms. Magazine* article titled "The Daring Escapade of 1916." It was written by Anne Tully Ruderman, Adeline's daughter who, incidentally, was listed in the 1983–84 edition of *Who's Who of American Women*. One sentence in the brief story states: "They were arrested a half-dozen times, too, in small towns between Chicago and the Rockies—for wearing men's clothes—but each time they were released with only a reprimand, provided they got out of town fast."

If an author unrelated to the family had written that article sixty years after the fact, and had taken some literary license to make the story more compelling, one might understand the embellishment. But Ms. Ruderman was Adeline's daughter, so it is reasonable to believe that she had heard of these incidents from her mother.

In the dozens of newspaper and magazine articles preserved in libraries and newspaper archives across the nation, I saw not a single reference that in any way suggested even a brush with the law, let alone arrests. In the many interviews the sisters gave during and after their journey, not one word hinted that they had had run-ins with the police, and certainly nothing indicates that they had been placed under arrest.

Admittedly, the word "arrest" means somewhat different things to different people. Someone who is stopped and questioned by an officer might call that action an arrest, while another person would consider arrest to mean physical custody—at a minimum being detained and taken to the police station for further questioning.

Certainly the sisters had regular interaction with the police as they passed through many small towns. They sought out contact with townspeople and newspapers, after all, on behalf of the Preparedness Movement. But small towns in rural America were very insular places in 1916, with attitudes to match.

One can reasonably conclude that a village police officer, having perhaps never, or only rarely, seen motorcyclists, would have stopped them and sought identification and information as to their intentions. That was to be expected; the presence of strangers in small towns a century ago didn't go unnoticed. Two female motorcycle riders dressed completely in leather most certainly would have attracted the attention of the rural gendarme. But nothing in the contemporary press suggested that those interactions went beyond the routine. Perhaps Ms. Ruderman was referring to these kinds of encounters when she wrote of the six arrests. We may never know for certain.

THE SISTERS RETURNED to New York City that Fall proud of their accomplishments and satisfied that they had done all they could to

The sisters take a well-deserved break on a California hilltop after completing their arduous cross country journey. (Photo used with permission of the Van Buren family)

spread the Preparedness message. They had confirmed a place in the record books for their Pikes Peak run and their solo motorcycle rides across the continent by women. Their success certainly eliminated any possible doubts about their resourcefulness and abilities.

Upon their return, the sisters applied to the Army to serve in the volunteer dispatch rider corps that was being organized. With every passing week, it seemed more likely that the country would enter the war, and motorcycle dispatch units were forming across the nation.

Some local preparedness units did record Adeline and Augusta as dispatch riders, the only women in the nation to be so listed. But in 1916 the U.S. Army wasn't accepting women in the military, especially if it meant being close to combat, and turned down their requests to serve.

It would be unfair to criticize the American military establishment, with the hindsight of a century later, for disallowing Adeline's and Augusta's enlistment requests. Men making those decisions were from an era where such an assignment would have been unthinkable. These protective attitudes were not unique to army officers. Post-Victorian society, including women as well as men, opposed ideas or policies that would place women in dangerous front line or trench warfare situations.

The men of the military establishment did allow some women to enter their world. During World War I, 13,000 women enlisted in the U.S. Navy, mostly doing clerical work. These women were the first in American history to be granted military status. The Army hired female nurses and telephone operators to work overseas as civilian employees in uniform.

However, the War Department did not approve recommendations to create a women's auxiliary corps such as Great Britain formed in January 1917, to perform clerical, supply, and communications work. The department also refused to commission female doctors in the Medical Corps.

THE AMAZING STORY of the sisters by no means ends with their arrival back in New York City. In fact, much remains to be told about these extraordinary women. They did return to their respective jobs, Adeline as an elementary school English teacher and Augusta as head of a stenographic unit in a large business. But they remained very active in the local motorcycling scene and continued their fight for the Army's recognition.

Given what they had already endured and accomplished, no one doubted their toughness, but the sisters continued to challenge themselves. Augusta was part of a two-person team, using a sidecar-equipped motorcycle, who won first place in a New Year's Eve endurance run. The race began at midnight on January 1, 1917, and ran 150 bone-numbing miles round trip between New York City and Poughkeepsie.

Thirty machines, twenty-four with sidecars, departed at set intervals from Columbus Circle in the city. They rode north on the Post Road, stopping at check points and keeping to a prescribed schedule and timing. Only eighteen machines finished, returning to the city in the wee and frigid hours of the morning. Of these eighteen, only two had perfect scores, including the team of Calvin Webber, operating a 1917 Powerplus Indian with Augusta Van Buren as his sidecar passenger.

The Hendee Manufacturing Company made full use of this victory in its advertising. A two-page ad in the next edition of *Motor Cycle Illustrated* tells the story very well.

> "At the stroke of midnight, with the church bells booming and whistles blowing in honor of the dawn of a new year, Indian began its string of 1917 triumphs in an impressive manner. With a bitter wind blowing in their faces, a wind which held a threat of snow in the air, thirty motorcyclists lined up for the Midnight Run between New York and Poughkeepsie and return.
>
> "All through that biting-cold night these intrepid riders, many of them accompanied by sidecar passengers, made their way. Past Peekskill, where the road is bared to icy blasts that sweep across the Hudson, along roads frozen into cement-hard ruts, into Poughkeepsie. Then back again, over the same heart-breaking roads, with the same searching cold now transformed into a sleety gale. Out of this terrific test, the most severe winter run attempted for many a year, emerged the Indian–the victor as usual."

Adeline also continued her love of riding and her loyalty to the Indian brand. On a frigid day in December 1916 she participated in the Yonkers Hill Climb. She claimed third prize on an Indian Featherweight, a lighter machine better suited for such competitions. It was the first time she had used the machine, so winning third place was quite an accomplishment.

On February 22, 1917, the large Indian agency in New York—Baker, Murray & Imbrie—hosted Indian Days. Over 600 enthusiasts showed up at the distributorship, despite the dead-of-winter weather. The event featured special speakers, demonstrations, vendors selling various items, and displays of the latest machines.

One highlight of the day was the arrival of Adeline, who had ridden 30 miles through snow covered roads on her trusty Indian motorcycle. Her fellow motorcyclists reportedly gave her a richly-deserved warm welcome. And well they should have! Perhaps only dyed-in-the-wool motorcyclists who have ridden in frigid temperatures and on snow-covered roads can truly appreciate the level of pure toughness needed to make that long ride down New York's frosty streets, or to participate in the local hill climb competition on a clear, very cold day two months earlier. No one could ever claim that these hardy sisters were posers or warm weather riders.

In April 1917, within days of America's official entry into World War I, both women rode to Springfield, Massachusetts, one more time. Their purpose was to spend time at the Hendee Manufacturing Company factory to learn first-hand how to perform advanced mechanical repairs on Indian motorcycles. They undertook this higher level training opportunity at their own expense and on their own initiative.

As was the case in many of their previous endeavors, the underlying reason for this additional education was to further qualify them for military dispatch duties. It seems likely that this training was in response to the Army's January 1917 letter to motorcycle clubs, urging members to receive special training to prepare them for possible duties in the military.

Once again confirming their desire to serve their nation in war time, the sisters told a Springfield newspaper reporter: "We don't know just what we may be considered competent to do. But whatever it is, we are ready and anxious to do our part to the best of our ability."

JULY 1917 ONCE again found the women on a lengthy motorcycle trip, but this time it was Canadian roads that they explored. Though I can find no record to document the exact route of their trip north, it's not far-fetched to imagine the sisters stopping at Laconia, New Hampshire, on their way to Canada to participate in the first ever FAM-sanctioned "Gypsy Tour."

Today, the Laconia rally is one of the largest and most popular motorcycle events in America, but its origins were more humble. It all began in 1916 when about 150 local riders converged on Laconia following a ride on the marvelous scenic and twisting roads through the nearby mountains. Just a year later, the 1917 event was a well-planned and -publicized two-day gathering of motorcyclists from throughout the region.

The term "Gypsy Tour" was coined at the time to describe overnight rallies to which people rode from distant locations to enjoy motorcycling solidarity and fellowship. A central element of Gypsy Tours was the overnight stay. The camaraderie gained by telling tales of their adventures around campfires was, and remains, a key ingredient of these events.

Gussie and Addie told Montreal newspaper reporters in early July that they intended to see as much of Canada as possible before they had to return to New York in September. Their lengthy story made it clear that the sisters maintained their attitude about service to their country, though the world around them had changed a great deal in the year since their California trip.

They were unwavering in their attempts to convince the Army that women should be allowed to serve as dispatch riders or perform other military duties as needed, including flying. At this point, Augusta was bitten by the aviation bug and, in time, she would pursue that dream. America had been in the war for three months already, and it must have been becoming frustratingly clear that their campaign to convince the military to allow women to enlist for non-combat duties was not succeeding. However, this did not deter them from their message and their fight, and they made their arguments for participation in the war effort as doggedly to Canadian reporters as they had to American newspaper and magazine publishers.

The sisters told the *Montreal Gazette* that they also planned to visit Toronto, if the roads were passable, and Quebec. With the U.S. and Canada both deeply immersed in the brutal European war, this trip lacked much of the excitement and following of their 1916 transcontinental ride. But they were still attempting to spread the message of the role of women in the military, in patriotic support of their country.

It's DOUBTFUL THAT anyone who knew the Van Buren sisters would have questioned their ability to succeed in the professional world. Despite societal limitations placed on women in the World War I era, it's hard to keep a good woman down when she has the skills and intellect to achieve whatever goals she sets for herself.

While the sisters never lacked self-confidence, there is no question that their exploits atop their motorcycles only added to their intrinsic conviction that they could overcome obstacles of every sort if only they dared to attempt and tried their best. One didn't journey thousands of miles through difficult terrain, with uncertainties and possible unpleasant surprises over every hill, without developing the attitude and confidence that success was a reasonable expectation.

Self-reliance, the propensity to try regardless of the odds, and confidence in her abilities derived from a lifetime of daring to push the limits helped Adeline Van Buren in the pursuit of her life's ambitions. She was a school teacher before and after her trips of 1916 and 1917, and I'm sure that she was a very effective one. Her students must have been in awe of this marvelous woman, who was barely taller than most of the children she taught, but who had gone on such incredible adventures. Her name was frequently in the papers because of the sisters' active lifestyle, and this must have fascinated the lucky youngsters who learned to conjugate verbs, diagram sentences, and speak proper English from Miss Van Buren. Motorcycle-riding English teachers were just not a common fixture in America's schools in the 1910s. I think the children learned many lessons, besides English, from this well-traveled and well-rounded teacher.

But Addie thought that perhaps she could do even more with her life, so she took a large leap into the world of higher education. According to university records, as the result of placing near the top on a competitive examination, Adeline received a "Chancellor's Certificate" from New York University's Woman's Law Class on April 6, 1918. The Certificate qualified her for a University Prize Scholarship of $360, covering tuition for the evening division of the Woman's Law Class, in which she enrolled in the fall of 1918.

RECEIVING THE CHANCELLOR'S Certificate and University Prize Scholarship was no paltry achievement. Earning the certificate was dependent on scoring highest on examinations given to prospective students. Adeline was one of only 23 young women who scored high enough on what was called the Chancellor's Examination to qualify for this enviable award. In addition to attending law school, Adeline continued teaching for many years. Her name appears in various newspaper articles in connection with her teaching position over the next decade, but I found no evidence that she became involved in a legal career.

In 1925 she married James J. Tully, who was also a public school teacher in the city. Their daughter Anne was born in 1927. Busy being a wife, a school teacher at Elementary School #34 in the Bronx, and a mother, there is no evidence of Adeline riding motorcycles beyond this point in her life. James and Adeline continued to live in New York City where she died, much too young, in 1949.

Augusta's interests also expanded as the years went by. Her 1917 dream of getting into aviation became a reality, and she received her pilot's license in 1924. She eventually joined Amelia Earhart's 99ers organization; an association formed in 1929 to advocate for the interests of female aviators. She remained an active pilot and belonged to the 99ers until her death, according to records at the organization's museum. During this period she also instructed others, including family members, how to fly.

Gussie flew her own plane around the country for pleasure as well as to attend 99er conventions. She also never gave up fighting to get the military to recognize the valuable services women could provide as pilots and in other military service roles.

In July 1941, when America was on the verge of entering yet another world war, Augusta flew her plane from New York City to New Mexico. There she was part of an Albuquerque gathering at which women pilots met with one of their own, Jacqueline Cochran. Miss Cochran had experience ferrying bombers to England as part of the British Air Transportation Auxiliary.

Cochran and two dozen other American women pilots had to join a British organization in order to perform what they considered as their patriotic duty. The 99ers felt that the many licensed women pilots in America could, at a minimum, provide a vital service to the Army Air Corps by flying planes from the factories to bases in America and overseas. The Madison, Wisconsin, *Capital Times* reported that Miss Cochran told them that, if she could handle a large bomber, being short and weighing only 117 pounds, then it was ludicrous for military officials to claim that women were not strong enough to handle the various military airplanes.

Ever so slowly, the military establishment had begun loosening its strict barriers against females doing anything other than medical or clerical work in the armed forces. By 1939, women were allowed to be part of the Civilian Pilot Training Program, which was geared toward national defense.

Cochran lobbied Eleanor Roosevelt in 1940, pushing for a women's division of the Army Air Corps to transport planes from manufacturing plants to military bases. A short time later, Nancy Harkness Love was successful in establishing the Women's Auxiliary Ferrying Squadron, and a few women were recruited to fly in that organization. Jackie Cochran returned to the states to establish the Women's Flying Training Detachment.

On August 5, 1943, these two programs were merged to become the Women Airforce Service Pilots, with Cochran as director. More than 25,000 women applied for the opportunity to serve in it, with requirements including a pilot's license and many hours of experience. The women had to pay their own way to the training in Texas, and the first class graduated on December 17, 1943. Of the 1,830 women accepted into training during WASP's existence, 1,074 graduated. The women were trained according to standard Army requirements, and their graduation rate was similar to that for male military pilots. While Augusta was not an Airforce Service Pilot, she no doubt took great pride in its creation and of her role in helping make it a reality.

While it existed, WASP pilots flew 60 million miles on missions, and 38 of them died. However, the group was never formally considered a part of the armed forces, and those who served were classified as civil service employees. Considerable opposition to the WASP program appeared in the press and was voiced in Congress, and it was deactivated December 20, 1944.

The WASP's records were classified and sealed, so the value of these female pilots was not fully appreciated for many years. In 1977, the same year the Air Force graduated its first female military pilots, Congress granted veteran status to those who had served in the program, and in 1979 issued official honorable discharges to the program's members.

Augusta Van Buren married Irving Roberts and, for many years, continued to live in the Bronx. Irving was the manager of a stock brokerage company, and she left her previous job and joined her husband as a telephone operator in the firm. At this point in her life she pursued flying rather than riding.

The Roberts later moved to a farm in Delaware where they lived out their lives and where Augusta was perhaps at her happiest. She was a country girl at heart, and she greatly enjoyed the open spaces of the rural area. Gussie was a down-to-earth woman who derived pleasure from outdoor activities, was proficient in the use of firearms, and who appreciated the freedom to get her hands dirty once again by raising crops and animals on their farm. She died in 1959 at the age of 75.

A century after their historic journey, the Van Buren sisters enjoy more recognition and appreciation for their deeds than they received in 1916. Many decades passed before these women received official accolades for their accomplishments. In 2002 they were inducted into the American Motorcyclist Association's Hall of Fame. A synopsis of the women's deeds, prepared by the Hall for the induction ceremony, sums up their life stories very well. A brief portion of the documentation reads:

> "Their lives were marked by a series of accomplishments. They were bright, enthusiastic, and refused to be held down by the limitations that society placed on women of that era."

In 2003 the sisters were also inducted into the Sturgis Motorcycle Hall of Fame.

Today many women understandably look up to Adeline and Augusta, as well as the other women featured in this book. All of them succeeded despite a societal deck stacked against them. They relied on their own wits and abilities to pursue a goal and prove that it could be done. They didn't set out to be role models for American women, but they are just that. It would be hard to find better examples for young women of the twenty-first century than these cutting-edge achievers of the early twentieth century.

Epilogue

—◦◦◦—

Many young women today proudly point to the subjects of this book as proof of what a determined woman can do, especially as their marvelous stories have become better known in recent years. Della, Effie, Avis, Adeline, Augusta, and the other women whose stories I've told would be at the same time humbled and proud. I'm sure they would tell us that they had never set out to change the world, but rather that they were doing only what their heart was telling them to do. And that is a simple yet powerful lesson: Following our dreams is an important thing to do, and in so doing we often learn that our dreams aren't ours alone; they belong to everyone.

An impressive array of women has followed the trail blazed by these and other pioneers by pursuing their own dreams in subsequent years. In many ways, the women who have stepped through the doors opened by those who came before them have left legacies equally important and impressive. The heritage of enthusiasm and can-do attitude of these latter-day pioneers is still visible today.

For example, Bessie Stringfield, an African-American woman, traveled extensively across North America in the 1930s and 1940s, enduring and overcoming the racial barriers of the time that sometimes put her life in jeopardy. Bessie achieved the Van Buren sisters' dream of serving as a dispatch rider for the Army during a time of war. As a civilian, Bessie was the only female motorcyclist to carry secret documents between military bases in America during World War II. The "Motorcycle Queen of Miami", known simply as BB to

197

her many friends, wore out 28 machines during her more than sixty years of riding.

Dorothy "Dot" Robinson carried the banner for women motor-cyclists in many ways: as a rider, owner of a dealership in Saginaw, Michigan, and as a very serious and able competitor. In 1935 Dorothy and her husband Earl set a record for a transcontinental ride from Los Angeles to New York City in less than 90 hours using a motorcycle and sidecar rig. Because Earl was ill, Dorothy did much of the driving. She was the first woman to win an AMA-sanctioned national event when she captured the sidecar category of Michigan's famed Jack Pine Enduro in 1940. After this victory Dot took on a larger struggle on behalf of female competitors. The American Motorcycle Association, as it was then called, did not recognize Dot's enduro victory because she wasn't a male competitor. Undeterred by such blatant discrimination she began a petition drive. She hand-delivered petitions with thou-sands of signatures to the association's headquarters and they relented, changing the rules and thus opening yet more doors for female riders and competitors.

Dot and her good friend and fellow rider, Linda Dugeau, crossed the country in 1939, seeking other women riders to establish an orga-nization for female motorcyclists. They formed the Motor Maids in 1940, and the club exists to this day, uniting women who have a pas-sion for two-wheeled adventures.

Robinson came by her love of motorcycling honestly. When her mother went into labor James Goulding, her father, loaded mother and daughter-in-waiting in their motorcycle sidecar and rushed across the Australian countryside to a hospital. Eighty four years later Dot was still riding! The Gouldings moved to America in 1918 and settled eventually in Saginaw, Michigan, where they opened a dealership. It was at this shop that future husband and motorcycle competitor Earl would stop in on a near daily basis, even if he didn't have a reason, and the rest is history.

Both Bessie and Dot were later inducted into the AMA Hall of Fame. Many other women continued the pursuit of motorcycling for pleasure, business, and competition. Women such as petite Vivian Bales, who became famous as Harley-Davidson's "Enthusiast Girl;" Easter Walters, actress and stunt rider; Lillian and Jane Farrow of the well-known and highly-respected Ohio family that ran the country's oldest Harley-Davidson dealership for decades. We could add dozens of others to this list.

Today, women comprise close to 15 percent of the total number of motorcycle owners. Many more enjoy the sport with husbands or friends. Dozens of clubs and organizations now exist solely for the purpose of providing support and camaraderie for women bikers. These groups range from traditional and quite formal organizations such as Motor Maids, to those that cater to road racers in their full leather racing gear. Thanks to the daring efforts of female riders of a century ago, the barriers that kept women from fully participating in motor sports have fallen.

We have come an amazingly long way since those exhilarating years prior to America's entry into "The War to End All Wars," when so much was new and exciting, and chasing dreams seemed very possible. Many alive at the time actually dared to dream that WWI would, in fact, be the war to end warfare forever.

With the taming of the geographic frontiers, the nation has had to look elsewhere, much farther away, to find new frontiers to conquer. No longer is simply driving across the continent, or even around the world, challenge enough. We have progressed immeasurably in issues such as women's rights and civil rights in general. Our technological advances have been nothing short of incredible, beyond even some of the most daring predictions of 20th century futurists.

It is all too easy to forget that, not all that long ago, things were very different in America. That the expressway-laced countryside and uncountable miles of pavement didn't exist less than a century ago, that women couldn't vote nor serve in the military, and that thousands died from polio, influenza epidemics, and other communicable diseases for which we now have vaccines or cures. Basic and universal civil rights were ideals that many fought for, knowing they would not live to enjoy them but hoping their children would.

Recent events of astounding historic importance and impact may cause us to think of the world only as it has existed in the past few years or decades, not as it was a century or more ago. It is tempting to ignore those developmental years, but that would be a mistake. As a society we learned important lessons in our early years, and the people and events behind those lessons shaped our nation and made us who we are. Those formative events, people, and years must not be forgotten lest we lose appreciation for the lessons learned through much work and pain.

We ought also to remember and honor those who, by their ideals and actions, created the mystique and legends of the American spirit. Those people's actions, like those of the many women whose stories appear in this book, helped establish an unshakable trust in an underlying indomitable spirit that has guided this nation since its founding. It is they, not we, who deserve the credit for the foundation of principles and can-do attitude that exists today. Our story is yet to be written.

Noteworthy Events: 1885–1925

1885	German engineer Gottlieb Daimler invented the modern gasoline engine with gas injected through a carburetor.
1885	The first "motorcycle" was built by Gottlieb Daimler. He called it a Reitwagen (riding carriage).
1891	The first concrete paved street in America built in Bellefontaine, Ohio.
1893	The Duryea brothers manufacture the first gasoline-powered automobile in America.
Nov. 28, 1895	America's first automobile endurance road race held near Chicago. Won with an automobile built by the Duryea brothers.
1897	Hendee Manufacturing Company established.
1898	Metz Company manufactures the first motorcycle in America.
Nov. 3, 1900	First automobile show in America, held in New York City's Madison Square Garden
Jan. 10, 1901	First major find of crude oil in Texas.
Jan. 22, 1901	Queen Victoria dies after a reign of 64 years.
May 10, 1901	Hendee Manufacturing builds their first true motorcycle.
Sept. 6, 1901	President McKinley shot by anarchist in Buffalo, NY.
Sept. 14, 1901	McKinley dies; Vice President T. Roosevelt sworn in as President.
Dec. 12, 1901	First trans-Atlantic radio signal broadcast.
1902	Bonneville Coventry, Ltd. formed—forerunner of Triumph Motorcycle Company.
Jan. 1, 1902	First Rose Bowl game played (Michigan vs. Stanford).
Mar. 4, 1902	American Automobile Association formed.

Aug. 22, 1902	Theodore Roosevelt is the first president to ride in an automobile.
1903	Harley-Davidson Motor Company formed.
May 16, 1903	George Wyman departs San Francisco on a motorcycle for the first cross-country trip using a motorized vehicle.
May 23, 1903	First automobile leaves the West Coast to make a cross-country trip to New York City.
June 16, 1903	Ford Motor Company founded by Henry Ford.
Sept. 7, 1903	Federation of American Motorcyclists, a lobbying and event sanctioning organization, is formed.
Sept. 11, 1903	First automobile race at the Milwaukee Mile.
Oct. 1, 1903	First modern World Series played (Pittsburgh vs. Boston).
Dec. 7, 1903	Orville Wright makes first controlled, powered flight in a heavier-than-air machine.
1904	First speeding ticket issued by police.
May 5, 1904	The United States begins work on the Panama Canal.
July 21, 1904	First automobile to exceed 100 mile per hour (in Belgium).
May 15, 1905	Las Vegas, NV, is founded.
April 18, 1906	San Francisco earthquake—over 3,000 killed.
Dec. 14, 1906	First German U-boat enters service.
1907	First telephone directory in the U.S.
Nov. 16, 1907	Oklahoma admitted into the Union as the 46th state.
1908	First Ford Model T manufactured.
April 1, 1908	First policewoman hired in America—Portland, OR
June 9, 1909	Alice Ramsey and friends leave New York City departing on cross-country trip in an automobile.
Aug. 2, 1909	The U.S. Army purchases first-ever military airplane.

Aug. 10, 1909	Alice Ramsey arrives in San Francisco, becoming the first woman to drive a car completely across America.
Sept. 2, 1910	Blanche Stuart Scott is first American woman to fly an airplane.
Jan. 18, 1911	First landing of an airplane onto the deck of a ship— on the deck of the USS *Pennsylvania* in San Francisco harbor.
May 30, 1911	First Indianapolis 500 race.
July 24, 1911	Fabled lost city of Macchu Picchu rediscovered in Peru.
1912	First motorcycle in America to exceed 100 mph
Jan. 1, 1912	Republic of China founded.
Jan. 6, 1912	New Mexico admitted to the Union as the 47th state.
Feb. 14, 1912	Arizona admitted to the Union as the 48th state.
March 1, 1912	First parachute jump from an airplane.
April 15, 1912	The RMS *Titanic* sinks in the north Atlantic Ocean.
April 20, 1912	Fenway Park in Boston and Tiger Stadium in Detroit open.
Oct. 31, 1913	The Lincoln Highway is formally dedicated.
Dec. 1, 1913	The world's first moving assembly line begins operations at a Michigan Ford Motor Company plant.
1914	Erwin "Cannonball" Baker rides a stock Indian motorcycle across the country in eleven and a half days.
Jan. 7, 1914	First steamship passes through the Panama Canal.
June 23, 1914	Delle Crewe leaves Waco, TX, on her motorcycle journey.
June 28, 1914	Archduke Ferdinand and Duchess Sophie shot in Sarajevo, Serbia.
July 11, 1914	Babe Ruth plays in his first professional baseball game.

Aug. 3, 1914	World War I begins in Europe.
Oct. 5, 1914	First aerial combat "kill."
1915	First coast-to-coast, long distance telephone line installed.
May 3, 1915	Effie and Avis Hotchkiss leave New York City for West Coast.
May 6, 1915	Babe Ruth hits his first home run.
May 7, 1915	A German U-boat sinks the RMS *Lusitania*
May 8, 1915	A horse named Regret was the first filly to win the Kentucky Derby.
Oct. 12, 1915	Effie and Avis Hotchkiss return from their cross-country round trip.
1916	Mexican guerillas cross the border and attack several American cities.
Mar. 15, 1916	General Pershing leads U.S. Army forces into Mexico.
July 5, 1916	Van Buren sisters leave New York City for the West Coast.
Sept. 2, 1916	Van Buren sisters arrive in San Francisco.
Sept. 29, 1916	John D. Rockefeller becomes worlds' first billionaire.
April 6, 1917	The U.S. declares war on Germany, entering World War I.
April 21, 1918	Manfred Von Richtofen (The Red Baron) is shot down over France.
Nov. 11, 1918	Armistice ends World War I.
Jan. 17, 1920	Prohibition, the 18th Amendment to the Constitution, takes effect—American goes "dry."
Aug. 18, 1920	The 19th Amendment ratified—guaranteeing the right to vote regardless of gender.
1923	Bayerische Moteren Werke (BMW) builds its first motorcycle.
1925	Federal highway numbering system developed.

Reference List

—◦◦◦—

Newspapers
Albuquerque Journal (NM): July, 1941
Berkeley Daily Gazette (CA): October, 1916
Boston Daily Globe (MA): March, 1915
Brooklyn Daily-Eagle (NY): October, 1915
Buffalo Evening News (NY): July, 1916
Capital Times (WI): July, 1941
Carbon County News Advocate (UT): August, 1916
Chester Times (PA): December, 1911
Chicago Tribune (IL): July, 1916
Chronicle Express (NY): January, 1955
Colorado Springs Gazette (CO): August, 1916
Daily Nonpareil (IA): July, 1916
Des Moines Daily News (IA): July, 1916
Deseret Evening News (UT): August, 1916
Elyria Evening Telegram (OH): December, 1913; January, 1915
Elyria Republican (OH): June, 1910; August, 1910.
Erie Daily News (PA): July, 1916
Evening Tribune (MN): June, 1915
Grand Junction Daily Sentinel (CO): August, 1916
Hamilton Daily Republican News (OH): June, 1915
Hartford Courant (CT): January, 1915
Hutchinson News (KS): July, 1914; March, 1915
Indianapolis Star (IN): January, 1915
Logansport Tribune (IN): September, 1916
Mansfield News (OH): November, 1915
Middletown Daily times-Press (NY): April, 1915
Milwaukee Journal (WI): April, 1915
Montreal Gazette (QC): July, 1917

National Democrat (IA): July, 1916
Nevada State Journal (NV): April, 1915; September, 1916.
New Castle News (PA); October, 1915
New York Sun (NY): November, 1915
New York Times (NY): March, 1912; May, 1912; September, 1914; October, 1914; November, 1914; December, 1914; May 1915; January, 1916; October, 1919; April, 1931.
Orange County Times-Press (NY); November, 1915
Oshkosh Daily Northwestern (WI); May, 1914
Pittsburgh Press (PA): August, 1916
Racine Journal-News (WI): August, 1914
Salt Lake Telegram (UT): November, 1915; August, 1916
Salt Lake Tribune (UT): September, 1915
San Francisco Call (CA); July, 1910
Springfield Daily Republican (MA): July, 1916
St. Louis Globe Democrat (MO): July, 1914
St. Louis Post Dispatch (MO): July, 1914
Syracuse Herald (NY): September, 1916; April, 1917
Terre Haute Star (IN): May, 1915; July, 1916
The Gleaner (Jamaica): May, 1915
Toledo Blade (OH): August, 1914
Toledo News Bee (OH): July, 1916
Wall Street Journal (NY); October, 1924
Washington Post (D.C.): June, 1914
Waterloo Evening Courier (IA): March, 1915
Wichita Daily Times (TX): July, 1914
Wyoming Tribune (WY): July, 1916

Magazines, Journals & Newsletters
American Defense Journal – 1916
American Motorcyclist – January, 1975
Antique Motorcycle – Summer, 2006
Effie Hotchkiss Journal
Effie Hotchkiss – Wheels In My Head
FTC Report on Price of Gasoline – April, 1917
Harley-Davidson Enthusiast – No. 1

Motor Cycle Illustrated – July, December 1916; January, February, March,
   April, 1917
Motor Cycle of London – 1914, 1915
Motor Way – September, 1901
Motorcycling & Bicycling – July, 1916
Motorcyclist – March, 1935
Ms. Magazine – February, 1978
New York University 1917/1918 Annual Catalogue
Ohio Public Health Journal - 1917
Popular Mechanics – November, 1915
Texaco Star – August, 1916

Books
A Century of Indian – Ed Youngblood; 2001
A Financial History of the United States – Jerry Markham; 2002
A Lady's Life in the Rocky Mountains – Isabella Bird; 1987
A Reliable Car and a Woman Who Knows It: The First Coast-to-Coast Auto Trips by Women – Curt McConnell; 2000
A Woman's World Tour in a Motor – Harriet Fisher White; 1911
Adventures of a Despatch Rider – Captain W.H.L. Watson; 1915
By Motor to the Golden Gate – Emily Post; 1916
The Lincoln Highway: Main Street Across America – Drake Hokanson; 1988
Order of Battle: The U.S. Army in World War I – Richard Rinaldi; 2005
The Rise of Theodore Roosevelt – Edmund Morris; 2001
The Sidecar Manual – Hal Kendall, 2003
Women Aloft: Epic of Flight – Valerie Moolman, 1981

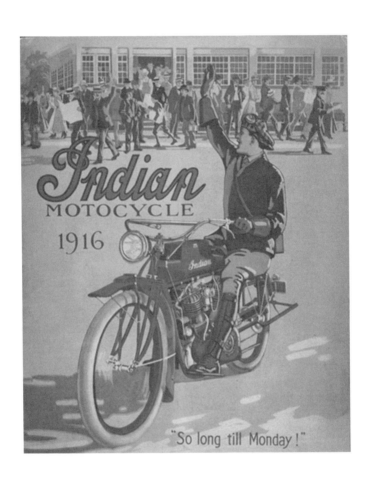